Broxbourne Centre Library 2C-EHC

Turnford, Broxbourne, Herts, EN10 6AE.
Telephone: 01992 411565

Please remember to return this item by the last
date shown below. You can extend the loan by
telephoning the library. *797.2♣ JUB*

A fine is charged for each item which is
returned late.

Dedication

To Edward and Charlotte, for all the enjoyment of our shared times.

Thanks

To Nick Juba and Dr David Hunt.

Published in 2006 by A & C Black Publishers Ltd
38 Soho Square, London W1D 3HB
www.acblack.com

First published in 2001 as *Fitness Trainers:
Swimming for Fitness*

Copyright © 2006, 2001 Kelvin Juba

ISBN-10: 0-7136-7391-5

ISBN-13: 978-0-7136-7391-3

A CIP record for this book is available from the British Library.

Note: While every effort has been made to ensure that the content of this book is as technically accurate and as sound as possible, neither the author nor the publisher can accept responsibility for any injury or loss sustained as a result of the use of this material.

Acknowledgements
Cover photograph © Getty Images
Photographs on pages vi, 4, 16, 44, 102 and 116 © Getty Images. Photograph on page 86 © Comstock. All other photographs © Grant Pritchard.
Illustrations by Jean Ashley
Cover and inside design by James Watson

Printed and bound in Dubai by Oriental Press

Contents

Introduction

Swimming as an activity has probably been around as long as man. Examples of man swimming can be found in a number of ancient documents and hieroglyphs, emphasising the enjoyment the sport has brought to people over thousands of years. The key difference between swimming as a sport now and swimming all those years ago lies in the reasons for taking part. Whereas years ago man swam for enjoyment, to fight wars and hunt for food, now we have very different objectives. Over the last 100 years, swimming has moved from being a sport associated with pleasure, competition or safety to one with a fourth and equally important objective – health and fitness.

Until the beginning of the 20th century, swimming was always referred to in books as being an art. Again, it is only over the last 100 years that it has been increasingly talked of as a science. In the following pages, it will be considered as both.

The 2002 General Household Survey recorded that 34.8 per cent of people had been swimming in the 12 months prior to being interviewed and that 13.8 per cent of people had been swimming in the previous four weeks. Of these, 30.3 per cent and 12.0 per cent respectively had taken part in indoor swimming. With the exception of walking, this exceeded the next most popular sport or physical activity by some 13 per cent. Given that 59.7 million people live in the UK, this would mean that 20.7 million people swam in 2002. The number of people swimming in the UK – a country surrounded by water – each year is enormous. The number is even greater when it includes people who swim in the sea or inland waterways. Swimming can proudly boast that it is among the top leisure pastimes in the UK, and much of this is due to the explosion in the number of people swimming for fitness. In adult competitive swimming alone, the level of interest is increasing. Some 8,130 people from 68 countries took part in the 9th World Masters Swimming Championships in Riccione in 2004.

More and more people are beginning to recognise the benefits of being fit in order to lead longer lives. A sensible diet, less stress and plenty of exercise are just a few ways of counteracting the pressures of modern life. Swimming very much fits within this. It is one of the few sports that can build stamina, flexibility and strength, while placing less strain on the heart because you can exercise without the additional burden of body weight. Swimming is also one of the few sporting activities that you can take part in throughout your life.

There are very few secrets in swimming. There are, however, many important ideas and handy hints to pass on that may help the general swimmer who wants to get fit or who is looking to maintain fitness. This book is directed towards those who belong to this group. It assumes that you already know how to swim, but that some updating may be necessary. Many of you who read this book may not have swum for many years. Remember, swimming can be great fun. Where else could you obtain such a high level of pleasure while truly benefiting in health terms? Let this book lead you down to the water! Come on in, the water's fun!

1 Why swim?

What is the difference between just swimming up and down a pool and swimming for fitness? If there is little difference between the two, why not just swim?

Swimming has a number of functions – pleasure, health and fitness and personal safety – and each of these is linked. If you swim for pleasure, you will almost inevitably develop some measure of fitness, however small. If you swim for health purposes, it is highly likely you will become fitter. If you swim for fitness, you will derive pleasure and are likely to be healthier. If you swim to become more confident in water, a degree of all three will rub off.

One major benefit of fitness swimming, however, is that it provides a structure to your swimming. This structure can promote variety and help you to plan your swimming in such a way that you get the most out of every one of your sessions throughout the year. Moreover, a well thought-

> **'Swimming is refreshing and revitalising – a wonderful pick-me-up at any time of the day!'**
>
> *Emily Wilson*

out programme of fitness swimming can help to ensure that you are doing the most beneficial things both at the right times of the year and within the same training session so that you achieve your objectives and get results.

Fitness benefits

Swimming is the perfect medium for improving fitness. It offers a warm and friendly environment not seen in most other adult sports. Because your body is beneath the water's surface, inhibitions about shape and size are removed, so even those people who are overweight need have no fears when taking part. On top of this, the extra support that water lends while you are exercising makes swimming a particularly beneficial approach to fitness training for many groups of people for whom land-based activities are less appealing or indeed impossible. In short, the barriers to entry are low.

Health benefits

Swimming can help people overcome and even prevent all sorts of illnesses and disabilities. Part of the reason for this is that water buoyancy makes it a non-impact form of exercise, removing the stress placed on the joints and therefore opening it up to people with a wide range of conditions for whom land-based activities are problematic. It is also a sport that exercises a wide range of muscle groups, builds muscular strength and endurance and develops self-confidence – the story opposite being a good example.

Weight loss

If you are taking up swimming to lose weight then you should aim to make it happen reasonably naturally. Put simply, to lose weight, you need to be burning more calories than you consume.

A regular diet supported by a steady programme of exercise should bring the body back to a suitable weight and body composition – basically how much body fat you have compared with muscle. Following the training principles set out in this book and eating a sensible diet (see Chapter 5) will allow you to lose weight sensibly and safely. However, you may feel that in taking up a swimming training programme, you actually need to gain muscle and

Duncan Newby, the national swimming coach to Bermuda and an active swimmer himself, was diagnosed as having oesophageal cancer while still young. Following an endoscopy in January 1998, he was told he had cancer and had to be operated on immediately. He was given a 2 per cent chance of survival, but with the help of friends and family he went to the most expensive cancer clinic in the world, the Memorial Sloane Kettering, New York.

The clinic told Duncan that the fact he had swimmer's lungs might give him a slim chance of survival. Throughout large courses of chemotherapy and radiation, Duncan continued to swim. Just three weeks after the operation, he swam in a 1300 m open-water race! And a few weeks later, he swam in a 4 km open-water race. This was despite the fact that Duncan had lost his stomach, oesophagus and part of his diaphragm.

Duncan's cancer is now in remission and he feels he owes his life to his swimming. In the summer of 2000, he swam a 10 km race in 2 hours and 55 minutes. He now plans to give talks in the UK about the wonders of swimming as a source of life extension and quality of life. This remarkable case of one man's determination to survive against the odds epitomises how swimming can help improve health even in the most serious cases.

therefore weight. For some people, gaining weight can be difficult, requiring them to eat large meals on a regular basis. However, the best way to gain weight is to increase muscular mass through a programme of strength training on land. This will stimulate and enhance muscle growth – active tissue that will enhance your swimming rather than gaining additional body fat, which may not. Either way, you should aim for gradual gain/loss; about 0.5 to 1 lb a week is a sensible target.

2 Getting started

Where to swim

Let us now consider some of the initial problems you might encounter, and where you can go to find out more in order to tackle them. (Contact details for all the bodies mentioned below can be found in the Further Information section on p 117–20.)

If you are having difficulty finding a suitable swimming pool, the leisure department of your local council should be able to make suggestions. If, however, this proves fruitless, you might like to contact the Institute of Sport and Recreation Management or the Amateur Swimming Association, who may be able give you further ideas.

Contact the pool you plan to swim at and find out when 'lane' swimming normally takes place. Pools have a variety of names they use for adult swimming, from 'jogging' to 'aqua fitness' to 'swimfit': try to find out when the pool is reasonably quiet and whether there is a resident group of adult swimmers who meet on a regular basis. The answers to

> 'Swimming not only uses all my muscles in one workout, but it is also a great stress reliever after a hard day at the office. There is nothing like gliding through the water, forgetting everything else around you, to ease away your troubles!'
>
> *Carrie Goldsworthy*

your questions will also probably tell you whether the pool management is reasonably sympathetic to adult fitness swimming. You will then be able to plan your swimming timetable. In doing so, look to the long term. Remember that the true benefits of your swimming programme will not be felt for a number of months. For more information on planning your swimming sessions, see Chapters 3 and 4.

Increasingly, swimming pool authorities have recognised the need for adult fitness swimming. Now whole lanes are set aside at certain times of the day or whole pools given over to fitness swimming. Unfortunately, in some pools this tends to only be carried out when requested by the public.

A 25 m pool is ideal, offering the opportunity to break your swim on a regular basis. Any longer, and this can be initially quite tiring for someone trying to regain fitness. Avoid pools that have poor shower, changing and toiletry facilities – this lack of attention may well be replicated in the way they look after pool water. Also, avoid pools where there is either a lack of discipline shown by the swimmers using the lanes, or where the etiquette of lane swimming is not recognised.

Most pools keep the outside, poolside temperature slightly higher than that of the water itself. Pools where the water is kept at a very high temperature are best avoided as they can make lengths swimming very uncomfortable.

If your difficulties are related to the content of your swimming sessions, it is probably best to contact the Institute of Swimming Teachers and Coaches at Loughborough. Alternatively, the Amateur Swimming Association has a Masters Swimming Committee directed towards adults.

Any medical problems or queries should be addressed in the first instance to your own GP, but if help cannot be obtained, the medical advisers at the ASA should be able to help you.

Kit

As with any sport, the right equipment is important. The main considerations are comfort and efficiency, and all kit should add something of both to your overall personal performance. Most of the items below can be bought from sports shops, leisure centres, swimming pools, websites or by direct mail. It may take trial and error for you to find the equipment that is right for you, but here are some handy hints that may prevent you wasting time and money in the first place.

Swimsuits

Enthusiastic swimmers never go anywhere without their swimming costume, just in case they have the time and opportunity for a quick swim. The swimsuit is obviously your most important piece of equipment, and you should aim to choose one that suits you with comfort and convenience in mind. Go for a swimming costume that doesn't trap air or water, and avoid a suit that rubs under the arms.

Nowadays, most swimming costumes are made of Lycra to reduce the effect of drag. The range of available swimwear has increased with fashion: the traditional suits have been supplemented with knee-length or full-body suits. Manufacturers state that the design of such suits has been achieved through biomimetics – in other words, they mimic various animals such as sharks. All of these suits are practical for the fitness swimmer and will dry quickly.

You will increase the life of your swimsuit by washing out pool chemicals. Sand, salt and suntan oils can also damage them. At the end of your day, soak your costume in ordinary tap water to preserve its condition.

Goggles

Lightweight goggles are common; some are better than others. Anti-fog goggles prevent misting. If you do find that your goggles mist up, lick the plastic eyepieces before putting them on. If you are not used to goggles, take care when putting them on to avoid eye injuries. Place the eyepieces over the eyes first. Then, while holding the eyepieces firmly over the eye sockets, pull the elastic band circuitously over your forehead and top of your head until the elastic band fits comfortably on the back of the head.

Swim caps

Most serious swimmers wear a latex hat to keep long hair out of their eyes, rather than to keep their hair dry. A swim cap can be particularly useful if you have to work after your swim. You may not get the time to wash your hair, and a latex hat will help to keep pool chemicals out of it so that you don't smell like a swimming pool while at work!

Nose clips

A nose clip is an optional piece of equipment used by some swimmers because they have difficulty in balancing the pressure of the air inside their nose with that of the water outside it. The clip normally consists of a 'U' shape that fits over the nose, with an elastic band holding it in place from the back of the head.

Earplugs and wraps

If you experience discomfort as a result of water getting into your ears, there are various types of self-moulding earplugs that you can buy from a chemist. Neoprene ear wraps can be used around the head to cover ears that are susceptible to invasion by foreign bodies.

'Because I've had two knee operations, for me swimming is a good way to keep toned as it's safer on my joints. I like to get a workout from swimming but I also find it very calming too. It's great after a busy day!'

Sarah Massie

Heart rate monitors

Heart rate monitors normally take the form of wrist watches, into which you can manually enter your heart rate data. The monitors can be set for different heart rate ranges or a specific number of beats per minute, and they indicate the percentage of your maximum heart rate at which you are working.

The more advanced versions will also indicate the number of calories you are burning, based on the intensity of your exercise. They will show you two versions – one based on the calories you are currently burning, and a second version based on the accumulated number of calories you have burned since the start of your swimming session. You can then take the heart rate monitor home with you and plug it into your PC to re-programme it ready for future sessions.

Logbooks

These will become a vital part of your overall planning. A logbook allows you to plan your schedules, keep a record of your training, and compare results over a period of time. It is, therefore, your swimming past, present and future!

In addition to the various items of personal equipment listed above, many pools make available training aids such as swim fins/flippers, pull buoys, hand paddles, kick boards, inner tubes and drag devices. Alternatively, you can always take these to the pool with you. A precautionary word, though – build up the use of such equipment very slowly. Too much too quickly, particularly with the arm-related equipment, can lead to aches and pains and sometimes tendinitis.

Joining a swimming club

If you weren't a member of a swimming club when you were younger, you might find the thought of joining a club fairly daunting. However, you need not be concerned – there is generally something for everybody. Nowadays, clubs take three forms: first, swimming clubs with their own separate section for Masters or adult swimmers; second, Masters clubs who cater for adult swimmers of any type; and third, those clubs who do not do anything for adults.

If you are contemplating joining a club, it is worthwhile making one or two phone calls beforehand. The first thing to decide is whether you want to take your swimming fairly seriously. If this is

The advantages of joining a swimming club

- You are likely to be swimming with people who share similar values and goals.
- A club represents an opportunity to swim on a more structured basis.
- There will be, more than likely, a coach to give you advice on your stroke technique.
- The group will have a clearly defined monthly and annual plan that you can work to.
- Group swimming helps to alleviate any boredom.
- At least part of the pool will be dedicated to adult lengths swimming.
- You will meet new friends and swimming colleagues.

the case, it might be better to join a club that enters Masters competitions. If, on the other hand, your main aim is to keep fit and have fun, then a club that spans all age groups and has an adult fitness session might be a better idea.

Your local swimming pool or leisure centre should be able to give you a better idea on what clubs have to offer. If, however, you are unable to obtain the information you need, contact the ASA Master's Committee Secretary (see page 117 for contact details) or contact the ASA Membership Services Department on 01509 618700. They will be able to give you some idea of the size of the adult sections of swimming clubs close to you.

It is important not to rush into joining. Make sure you find out more about the club before you start.

Medical advice

Before you embark on a training programme, it is a good idea to have a check-up with your general practitioner. Ask your doctor for

Questions to ask before joining a swimming club

- Does the adult session have a coach or teacher or does it run its own sessions?
- How long do the sessions last?
- How many lengths are you expected to do? How many lengths does the average adult swimmer complete?
- Does the group take part in Masters competitions?
- What is the cost?
- Does the group swim all year round?
- Does all the swimming take place at one pool or does the group ever travel away to swim?
- How many people on average turn up to swim each week?

a 'well person check-up' – these are free and will include a check on your heart and lung function. During swimming, your cardiac system will be called on to work hard and your blood pressure is a good indication of its condition. It is also a good idea to get your doctor to test the efficiency of your lungs, since oxygen consumption will be important to you when you get into training.

Also, ensure that your lifestyle begins to take account of a new training programme. Smoking harms the lungs' capacity to work efficiently while training and should therefore be reduced or given up. Alcohol should be limited to a maximum of 14 units per week for women and 21 units a week for men. Heart and lung fitness will become important elements in your swimming programme.

In general, common sense is the order of the day. If you are not over-weight and you are under 50 years of age, you can build gradually into a fitness swimming programme. If you are over 50, you should progress with extreme caution, avoiding over-extending yourself in the early stages. If in any doubt, always consult your doctor. The most important thing to bear in mind is that whatever your sex, ethnicity, age or state of health, you can take part in swimming for fitness. Swimming remains accessible to almost everyone.

Goal setting and motivation

Goal setting

Setting goals and objectives is highly recommended. It will help to keep your mind focused and will mean that you are less likely to retire at an early stage when the going gets difficult. A goal tends to be qualitative in nature, while your objectives are more likely to be quantified. In other words, your objectives will be more precise and more closely defined than your goals.

Let's consider objectives first. If you are a more serious swimmer, you will have time targets in mind. Your aim may be to swim 100 metres freestyle in 1:05.0 at the peak of your season in July. You can then work backwards, setting yourself small milestones on the way. For instance, you might be aiming to swim 1:10.0 in December, January and February when you are in harder training and 1:07.0 in April and May. You might even decide that the mini targets are useful but not essential as you strive to build up towards your 1:05.0 objective for the year in July.

However, if you are in the water mainly to get fit, you are likely to have different objectives. For instance, you might want to lower your blood pressure from 160/95 to 135/75 over a six-month period through relatively hard swimming, or to lower your resting heart rate or your recovery rate over the same period. Your objective is more likely to be about achieving a certain distance, such as 1500 m, in your half-hour swimming session, or alternatively to build up to an hour's swimming and aiming to swim 3000 metres in an hour by August, having started the previous November. Goals are a little different. Your goal might simply be to get in shape for the summer holiday, which would involve losing half a stone in weight over a nine-month period and attempting to improve your muscle tone. The whole sense of a goal is more long-term and more general. You need to be clear about what you want to achieve and set yourself a goal that you can realistically achieve in a given period of time.

Motivation

Despite having your head under water for much of the time when swimming, it is a great social sport, and this can help in your motivation. If you are returning to the swimming pool after a number of years, try to swim with a partner or a group of friends. Try to team up with someone who prefers the same stroke and is about the same speed. If possible, look for someone who shares the same goals as you. For example, if you want to get really fit and intend to swim four or five times a week, there is little point in starting out working with someone who won't be able to spare the time to train six months down the road.

Benefits of swimming with a friend or a group

- You can get a partner to look at your strokes and help you to correct any obvious technical errors you are making, both over and under the water.
- A partner to swim with and compete against while getting fit can make life much more interesting.
- You get a sense of teamwork, which makes the swimming mentally easier and more purposeful: there is a shared feeling that you are all 'in it together' and taking part in something worthwhile.
- You can use slipstream swimming: lane swimming often means chain swimming – in other words, following one another up on one side of the lane and returning on the other side of the lane. Swimming behind someone else in this way can give you distinct psychological encouragement.
- Having someone to talk to when you get to the end of a swim is a good chance to be sociable, as well as to create points of comparison and reference while training.

Keeping a training diary

A training diary can be a very useful tool for both the fitness and Masters swimmer. It can help you monitor your progress year on year, and also help you to plan and focus on what you are trying to achieve. And it takes literally five minutes each evening to write down what you did in your swimming session that day.

What, then, are the things that you need to record in your training diary?

1. Your 'medical' details:

- your resting heart rate (RHR)
- percentage body fat – a measurement you can find out from a physio or at a gym
- flexibility levels.

Update all of these every six months.

2. Your personal details: height and weight – bearing in mind that your body composition is more important than your weight per se.

3. Details of all training sessions: date, time of day, venue, the swims you have made, amount of rest between each rep (if any).

4. Targets and general records for each month:

- any target times set at the start of the month in training and then achieved
- any target times set at the start of the month for races and then achieved
- the distance you plan to swim
- how much time you plan to devote to your swimming
- an overall framework of sessions for the month.

> 'Let's be honest, swimming is a cheap way of exercising. It's accessible, reasonably comfortable and a good alternative to the gym.'
>
> *Jason Carpenter*

5. Mechanical details such as:

- number of strokes achieved by stroke counting at medium speed
- number of strokes achieved by stroke counting at maximum speed.

Eventually you may prefer to plan and write your own schedules before you train, rather than to plan the session in your mind, do it and write it up afterwards. It is a good idea to do this for all your

Swimmer's shorthand

Always try to write your swims in shorthand to make life easier, e.g. '4 × 100 back + 30 sec' rather than '4 × 100 metres backstroke with 30 seconds rest between each swim'.

monthly schedules, about two weeks beforehand. The difficulty, of course, is in sticking to them!

3 Training know-how

Planning your training

The first great problem you are likely to encounter when considering swimming for fitness is overcoming inertia. Modern life is comfortable and you may not want to break out of your routine. Be positive at the start. Once you have decided to commit yourself to getting fitter, plan one or two hours of regular swimming into your week. Try to plan the time of your sessions a month ahead and stick to it. In scheduling your swimming, try to avoid days when you already have other physical activities, family commitments and time pressures. For example, if you are going to swim for an hour then swim for an hour – not 45 minutes because you find you have to spend time drying your hair, putting on your clothes and getting back to an important meeting at the office.

Pushing yourself can be very difficult, but that's what any fitness programme requires. Your initial sessions will be all about acquainting yourself with the water, and the lengths you swim can be at a very easy pace. Recognise that a level of fitness will not be achieved without a

> 'I feel much better after an early morning swim. I'm much more alert at work and can concentrate more on what I'm doing.'
>
> *Janet Tanner*

certain amount of effort. Eventually, though, you will need to move out of this comfort zone and this is when your fitness programme will become harder – both physically and psychologically.

At this point, you will have the inevitable self-doubts: 'Why do I do this? Perhaps this isn't such a good idea after all. I think I prefer music or reading as a hobby – they are much less demanding at my time of life. Can I really keep this up?' Faced with this, set yourself realistic and achievable goals before you go to the pool and stick to them. If you have set yourself half an hour for your session, make sure you swim for half an hour, not 20 minutes! The right way to break out of your comfort zone is to attempt this in short stages. Build up your workload slowly; in time, your efforts will become easier as you get fitter and your body adapts to the increased level of exercise.

Easing your way back to fitness

The first session is going to be the most difficult part of any swimming programme. You are bound to feel a little stiff after each session, especially after the first few, but the level of stiffness will soon ease. If you are a little older, try to account for this in your planning by building up gradually. If you can swim with a friend or as part of a group this can really help to break down early barriers. To help record your improvements and achievements, buy a simple diary that you can use as both a log of your swimming sessions and a diary for future planning.

Gradual increases in levels of intensity should be the cornerstone of your swimming during the early months. Try to work at your own rate and bear in mind that sometimes you won't improve at all. You may stay at the same level or go back slightly before moving forwards to the next plateau. Your swimming actually becomes an act of faith as well as a matter of scientific and artistic approach. You have to believe that what you are doing will be beneficial in the long run.

The first session

Be prepared to ease your way back in with some very simple exercises, even if you have previously swum at quite a high level.

Before you get into the water, take your pulse (see pp. 34–5). After the session, you might want to record this in your swimming diary for future reference.

Then slide into the water off the pool deck. Avoid diving in the first time, since this almost suggests having to swim fast as soon as you leave the poolside. During this first session, you need to emphasise ease of movement. As you slide in, try to build up a mental picture that this is how you want to swim – you want your movements to be slippery, oily and fish-like when you start. Imagine that you are going to try to cut through the water with all your movements, and that you are going to move the water with a steady force that doesn't cause the water to splash. The last thing you want is heavy, over-emphasised actions that move your body all over the place in the water. These early mental pictures may seem fairly trivial but they will focus the mind on exactly how you are going to approach your swimming programme.

Then, from a standing position, push off from the bottom of the pool, stretch your arms together out in front of you and just glide. Do this a few times with your face in the water between your arms. Perhaps you had forgotten what it feels like to be back in a pool: this movement will help you to get used to the feeling of weightlessness and of having your face in the water, breathing out. Remember, there is no hurry at this stage to get swimming. Acquainting yourself with the water is just as important.

After doing this a few times you can try swimming some easy strokes. These would normally be freestyle or breaststroke, but you might want to simply keep your hands stretched out together in front of you and to kick legs-only on either stroke with your face in the water. Slide your hands into the water instead of 'crashing' them through the surface. Try to stretch out on the strokes and really try to feel the water as your hands pull. Your hands will tend to make sculling movements. Remember that at a certain point in the stroke – whatever that stroke is – you will keep the hand fixed in one plane while you pull your body past that fixed position, a little bit like watching a boat being rowed from one side. The efficiency of the sculling movement is therefore important.

> '**I like swimming because of the way my body glides through the water – it makes me feel extremely light and supple. It's also the most relaxing form of exercise I do – I love the fact that although you're working hard, there is no painful impact and no sweat!**'
>
> *Pippa Tordoff*

Take a break and then try kicking a length very steadily with your arms out in front of you. Then take another break and swim full stroke for a length. Try this about six times in all.

Stroke-counting is a handy way of getting used to using the water as efficiently as possible. In the first instance, it is much easier to count the number of strokes per length when you are moving slowly than when you are moving fast. Count the number of strokes it takes you to swim the length. Take a rest for about a minute at the end of the pool and try to do one less stroke on the way back. You might want to do this for half a dozen lengths and then record the results in your diary later, as they will set standards for the future.

Following this, loosen down with some easy, very relaxed swimming over about four lengths and that will be sufficient for this session. Keep the first few sessions at this level so that you can get used to the water and avoid too many early aches and pains. Eventually your body will adapt to increasing levels of exercise, but the intensity of your sessions needs to be built up gradually. If you fail to consider your body in this way, it could prove unproductive and demoralising.

Warming up and cooling down

It is now widely acknowledged that you should warm up the body before undertaking any form of exercise. This has the effect of preparing the heart, muscles and joints for the main part of the training session, and has several physiological and psychological benefits.

The warm-up should always be gradual. If done too vigorously, muscle glycogen is depleted, and lactic acid may be present at the start of a session. Build into your training programme without over-extending yourself at first.

Chapter 4 covers body conditioning – strength and flexibility work – in greater detail, but the following simple exercises are all that is required to help you prepare both mentally and physically for your fitness swimming programme. When you have got used to your quick routine, you may want to use two or three exercises only and to change these from session to session.

Essentially, the warm-up:

- increases the temperature of the muscles, which allows them to contract more rapidly and more forcefully, and to relax more quickly;
- causes a rise in general body temperature and a gradual lifting of the heart rate, opening up the capillaries and ensuring that sufficient blood is transported to the muscles to be exercised;
- stretches the muscles and loosens connective tissue;
- replicates the neuro-muscular patterns required in the training session;
- encourages the release of synovial fluid – the fluid that allows smooth movement of bone over bone – into the joint capsules, and warms the tendons and ligaments as well as the muscles that surround each joint. The joints are therefore well lubricated prior to use;
- prepares the swimmer mentally for the training session ahead.

A simple warm-up routine on land

If possible, make the time to perform a simple warm-up on the poolside before you start your swimming session. Don't expect too much of yourself at first – a few light exercises are sufficient. You should set aside about five minutes before each swimming session for stretching, particularly the shoulders and the ankles (see pp. 68–78).

Here are a few suggestions, each of which should last 15–30 seconds:

- Start by standing upright with your feet shoulder-width apart. Circle each arm through 360 degrees, or as near as possible. Take the right arm and circle it forwards several times; then, with the same arm, backwards. Repeat on the other side. In order to ensure that your body is vertical throughout, look immediately in front of you while circling. Carry out these movements quite slowly so that you can feel the complete range of movement at the shoulder joint. Keep your shoulders down and your back straight throughout.

- Now you can get the feel of swimming by draping your body forwards at the hips and mimicking the freestyle action. By now your shoulders should be getting used to the rotational movements, so you can make your freestyle arm movements that much quicker. Follow this by switching to butterfly arm movements. Keep your back straight and your head in alignment.

- The next stage is to stand upright again and circle your arms together backwards. The movement should be fairly slow, and when your hands reach the vertical above your head, your shoulder blades should feel as though they are going to scrape together. Again, ensure that your shoulders do not lift up during the exercise.

- Now raise your left arm and hold your elbow with your right hand. Press gently backwards to stretch the triceps at the back of the upper arm. Your head and body should remain vertical and you should face forwards throughout. Hold the stretch for 15–30 seconds and then repeat on the other side. A partner, if you have one, can help you keep the whole movement steady and controlled.

■ You are now ready to move on to another simple exercise, this time stretching the hamstring muscles at the backs of your legs. Place your towel on the ground and sit upright, with one leg  straight and the other comfortably bent out to the side. Bend forwards from your hips, reaching towards your toes until you feel a stretch at the back of your thigh. Keep your back straight and your head in alignment. Hold for 15–30 seconds and relax. Repeat on the other side.

■ Finally, bend your right leg and place your right ankle on your left thigh, above the knee. Holding your ankle with your right hand, rotate your foot with your left hand through 360 degrees.  When you have repeated this a few times, rotate in the opposite direction. Repeat on the other ankle.

Stretching in the water

Sometimes, easy stretching in the water is preferable to stretching on land. You may find, for instance, that there is little room on the pool deck – and during busy public swimming sessions, land-based exercise routines do not go down all that well with the bathing fraternity. In addition, some stretching in the water tends to get you used to the feel of steady resistance that you will encounter when actually swimming.

- Start by facing the side of the pool. Holding on to the pool deck or rail, place your feet flat on the wall and straighten your legs at the knees (incidentally, this is also a useful way of relieving cramp if you get it while training).

- Next, stand on the bottom of the pool and walk away from the shallow end towards deeper water. Push off the bottom of the pool by pressing down through your toes. Try this several times.

- Now, standing on the bottom of the pool, lift your knees one at a time. Try to get your knees as high as possible, preferably above your waist. As you change legs, try to bounce gently on your feet to add rhythm to the movement. Your forearms rest on the surface of the water throughout.

- Then stand on the bottom of the pool with your legs apart. Choose an appropriate depth so that your shoulders are level with the surface of the water. Extend one arm to the side in line with your shoulder. Move the hand of the other arm in an anticlockwise direction under the water surface, in one big arc in front of your body – extending your arm to its maximum. Your hand stays about 5 cm under the surface throughout. Your arm is then returned to the start position, and the exercise repeated on the other side. Try to accelerate the hand movement through the water so that the resistance of the water increases.

- Follow this by working on some side bends. Stand upright so that the water surface is beneath shoulder level. Keeping your arms by your sides, tilt your body to the right and slide the fingers of your right hand as far down the side of your right leg as possible. Repeat on the other side, making sure that you keep your hips in alignment throughout the exercise.

■ Now try water squats. Stand in chest-deep water with your feet turned out and slightly further than hip-width apart. With your hands on your hips, bend your knees in line with your feet, keeping your back straight and your head facing forwards. When your chin sits on the surface, straighten your legs at the knees. Repeat several times.

■ The last exercise requires strength as well as flexibility. Ease your way up to the deep end of the pool. Face the poolside and place your arms above your head in line with your shoulders. Press down with your hands on top of the poolside, pulling your chin and then your upper body out of the water until your hips are level with the poolside. Now allow your body to ease back to its starting position in the water. Do this four or five times to get the feel of the last phase of the pulling movements in freestyle and butterfly.

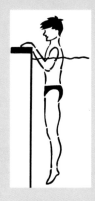 

The loosen-off or cool-down period is just as important as the warm-up. The main reason for the swim-down is so that all the body systems can regain their pre-training state. Blood needs to be returned to the heart in order for it to help in the removal of waste products such as lactic acid. Generally, lactate can be more rapidly removed when the muscles are working at a low intensity.

Lactic acid occurs naturally in the body as a by-product of exercise. It builds up when the muscles are tired or fatigued, and is brought about during the breakdown of the carbohydrate glycogen, when insufficient oxygen is available to the body. During the cool-down, muscular contraction brings about a squeezing effect on the veins, pushing venous blood back to the heart at an increased rate. At this point excess lactate is removed and metabolised by cardiac muscle fibres.

Just like the warm-up, your loosen-off period also has psychological benefits, helping to relax the mind and remove feelings of stress by the time you leave the water. This will promote a feeling of well-being at the end of your training session.

When planning your session, try to allow at least five minutes at the end to loosen off. This period will allow you to ease down, get rid of any carbon dioxide from your lungs and clear as much lactic acid from the rest of your body as possible. The longer and harder your session, the more time you need to fully loosen down. Most people find that their loosen-down will depend on the time they have available – but try not to skimp on it.

Loosen off with some easy freestyle or breaststroke (5–6 lengths), or by swimming legs-only very easily with the face placed in the water from time to time. All three of these will allow you to breathe out into the water, thus clearing the lungs. Arm recovery movements can be fairly floppy and the pull does not need to be strong. Hopefully you will have worked hard but won't leave the pool feeling like a wreck.

The swimming strokes

Now that you've made the initial breakthrough and are thinking of going back into the water, time spent brushing up on your strokes will help to keep you on the right track. It is important to get into good habits from the start, as faults tend to multiply as swimming becomes more intensive. Remember, speed has a direct relationship with stroke efficiency, not energy expenditure. One of the great difficulties in returning to a fitness programme of this nature lies in trying to build up a mental picture of what your strokes actually look like. Many people cannot remember what their technical faults were when they swam in the past; this is made harder by the fact that you can't see yourself while you are swimming, which is why exercising with a partner or in a group is of such value. If, however, you are swimming on your own and find it hard to visualise your own strokes, the following section offers some useful tips. It does not claim to be comprehensive but assumes that you have already reached a certain standard in your swimming – for example, the ability to swim 20–30 lengths in the past. There are many books that cover stroke technique to a high standard, and if you feel you would like to examine this in detail then the Amateur Swimming Association at Loughborough has a comprehensive publications department.

Focus on your technique

Concentrate on the basics: a good push-off; completing each stroke before going into the next one; using the neck and head to streamline the body and make it flatter on the surface of the water.

Freestyle

Freestyle, or front crawl, is the fastest of the strokes. The important thing to bear in mind at this initial stage is streamlining. Any undue lateral movement is going to cause an opposite reaction, which will mean that the body snakes from side to side.

Try to imagine that you are swimming down a tube about 1 m in diameter. Your main aim in all the movements is to avoid touching the side. To do this, your elbows need to be bent and held perpendicularly during the recovery of the arm. This can be achieved by aiming to show more and more of the armpit as the arm is recovered. Your fingers need to be relaxed as they face down towards the water's surface. When pulling under the water, your hands need to press back towards your stomach and then on towards your upper legs.

Swimmers employ a number of different rhythms for freestyle. These rhythms are governed by the number of leg-kicks for each arm cycle. Generally, six leg-kicks to each complete arm-cycle (i.e. completion of 360 degrees of movement by both arms) are used when a swimmer wants to swim at speed with a longer arm stroke. If you want to swim over a longer distance, a strong six-beat kick is too tiring to maintain and most people will revert to a four-beat, two-beat or a two-beat kick with a cross-over (where the legs move laterally to the side but do not complete a downward movement).

The two-beat kick consists of a downward kick by one leg as the opposite hand begins its pull. For example, the right hand sinks and sculls in the water to a point where it catches hold of the water at the start of the pull. At this point, the left leg is driven towards the bottom of the pool, partly as a form of balance and partly for propulsion. The opposite movements occur when the left hand enters.

The four-beat kick can involve a 'cross-over' of the legs. As with the two-beat kick, there are two downward movements; but there are also two downward involuntary kicks, which are made as a crossover so that during the downward movement, one leg-kick crosses at the knee of the other. The reason for this involuntary movement is simply to balance the body and counteract any lateral body movements brought about during the arm-cycle either by the arms, or by excessive breathing movements. For the purposes of fitness training, four or two leg-kicks for each leg-cycle are sufficient.

Breaststroke

While breaststroke is the slowest of the four competitive strokes, it is probably also the most relaxing. It particularly suits fitness swimmers who are exercising in busy public pools, as it allows a good view of other people in the water.

Breaststroke basically comprises a series of sculling movements, where you try to part the water with your hands for your head and body to pass through. The stroke begins with the legs straight; then bend the knees, with the heels lifted towards the backside. The feet fan out so that the soles face backwards in preparation for the kick. When the kick takes place, the feet move circuitously, the toes staying curled. The heels are brought together and the toes point at the last moment to produce a whipping movement.

During the pull, your arms stay in front of your shoulders, and your hands in front of the face. Your head is lifted at the end of the outward scull so that you can take a breath, with the exhala-

'Breaststroke is definitely the best stroke for me. I tend to swim during crowded public sessions as it's the only time I can get to the pool, and if I swim breaststroke, I can see more.'

Phil Pennington

tion taking place as the arms are straightened in front of the head during the kick.

Backstroke

Backstroke, or back crawl, was introduced in the third Olympic Games in 1904 and it remains an important stroke today, although the way in which it is swum has changed considerably. Now, the best backstrokers rely on a strong leg-kick, with the arms being driven back deep behind the head to increase the range of their pull. To achieve this, it is important to roll at the shoulders while keeping the head and the central vertical axis of the body as still as possible.

Backstroke is a bit like rowing a boat. Your hands start pulling from a position at arm's reach in front of your head. The hands pull until they 'fix' on the water almost in line with the shoulders, and then push the body past this fixed position. This action is then replicated with each arm-stroke.

In a similar way to freestyle, the legs can kick at the rate of six, four, two or two beats with a crossover movement to each arm-cycle. Again, a sprint version of backstroke normally calls for a six-beat kick, while if you are conserving your energy you will look for just two kicks to each arm-cycle. If you want to swim good backstroke, think about holding your head still enough to balance a glass of water on it while you are performing the stroke.

Butterfly

Butterfly is the most recent of the competitive strokes, being introduced in the 1930s. It will take you a number of weeks to work up to using this stroke as part of your fitness programme, but it is covered here in order to complete our short review of the strokes. Just as breaststroke reminds you of a frog, and freestyle and backstroke of a water-boatman, butterfly was referred to as 'butterfly dolphin' during its early years because of the similarity of the up-and-down movements to those of a dolphin.

The rhythm of the stroke is very important, and the most proficient swimmers aim to kick at either end of the pull. The weight of the head, coupled with the fact that both arms are simultaneously above the water for much of each stroke-cycle, can make the whole stroke very tiring. To facilitate these movements, try to get the timing right and avoid carrying the weight of the head out of the water for too long. You can work on this by following the 'two head before' rule: your head should go into the water before your arms enter, and come out of the water before your arms exit.

The best way to get into swimming butterfly is to lengthen the whole stroke out. Start by kicking legs-only under the water with your arms straight out in front of you, making long, easy up-and-down kicking motions. Eventually you can add the arms. When you start using your arms, avoid continuous rotation – introduce the stroke steadily by recovering the arms, holding them out in front of you before you pull and then adding an extra kick.

The building blocks of training

Basic training concepts

Whatever your fitness goal, you will need to train to achieve it. The process of training involves a number of basic concepts defined briefly here.

In simple terms, training involves subjecting your body to 'stress' and then allowing it to adapt so that it will be able to cope better with similar and increased stresses in the future. Swimming is just one of many ways in which the body can be positively stressed, resulting in the development of more efficient physiological systems.

Overload

This is a fundamental training principle dictating that fitness improves only when the demands placed on the body during training are greater than those normally encountered. For example, if you have been swimming regularly for the past few years but doing exactly the same thing each time you go to the pool, you will need to introduce some additional overload if you want to actually begin training.

The greatest fitness improvements are likely to come about when you begin to overload your energy processing systems (e.g. heart, lungs, circulatory system). The demands you place on your body under these conditions stimulate your body to adapt and, over time, to progress. You will know you are progressing when you can swim at maximum with a feeling of decreased effort. Normally this comes after several days of hard training followed by slightly easier training. Once you have progressed you can up your training to an increased level of intensity and the adaptation and progression process will start again, but this time at a higher level than before.

It is worth noting, however, that after initial overload the body will experience fatigue so that you won't necessarily experience positive feelings immediately. This is why rest is also a key aspect of training.

Overload can be achieved by manipulating the following three training variables:

- frequency – this simply refers to how often you are training. Research shows that for aerobic conditioning to occur you should be swimming three times per week;
- duration – this is defined as the length of time you are swimming at a particular intensity, either for the total time of the entire swimming session or via a series of repeated efforts (repetitions) with periods of rest between;
- intensity – this is basically how hard you are working and can be measured in terms of speed, heart rate and subjective feelings ('I feel better than I did when I finished training last week').

Monitoring your heart rate

Your heart rate is a useful indicator both of your general fitness and the overall progress you are making in your swimming programme, as well as providing a useful marker of the intensity you are training at when in the pool. Your pulse shows how fast your heart is working rather than how efficiently it is working. When you begin your swimming programme, your heart will work faster during any given swim than it will later, when you are fitter.

You can measure your pulse manually in three ways:

- by pressing gently with your middle finger on the carotid artery on one side of your neck; it is situated at the side of your head and approximately 3 cm from the bottom of your earlobe;
- by pressing your fingers on your heart;
- by pressing the middle finger of one hand on the inside of the other wrist.

Count the number of beats that your heart makes in 15 seconds, and then multiply this by four to obtain the number of beats per minute (bpm). This can be carried out at any time during your session to monitor whether you are training at the right intensity, but it's also useful to measure it at the start of your whole programme, to give you a baseline for future measurement.

As a general rule, an average person needs to exercise to a level whereby their heart rate sustains 150 bpm in order to really benefit.

That being said, it is important to note that your heart rate measurements relate only to you and to your performance; comparisons with other swimmers' results are not really relevant. Bear in mind, too, that an unusually high heart rate early in the session might indicate overtraining (see p. 43), or possibly the onset of an illness. In such a case, be careful to rest or adapt your training accordingly.

You should also take your pulse five minutes after exercise. If it is still around 120 bpm or noticeably elevated, your training has been too hard. Ten minutes after exercise your pulse should be below 100 bpm and heading towards the average resting pulse rate of 70 bpm. Your body's ability to adapt needs to be developed gradually; this guideline will help to indicate when you are trying to achieve too much too quickly.

Training cycles

The idea behind cyclical training is to provide periods where you can rest and regenerate – at certain times you will be swimming hard, but these are counterbalanced by substantial periods where you are not asking so much of your body. These periods of regeneration take place after intensive periods of hard training and they are considered necessary in order to guarantee continuous improvement. The periods employed vary from swimmer to swimmer but can include any-thing from 6- to 12-week cycles, with 3 weeks hard training followed by 6 weeks rest.

Longer cycles are known as macrocycles and are normally designed to fit in with the short-course and long-course swimming season described later in the book. They allow the swimmer to reach three or four peaks during the year. Microcycles refer to shorter periods lasting from a few days to one or two weeks. A mesocycle is a string of microcycles generally lasting for between two and seven weeks. The mesocycle always contains a period of hard work as well as an easier regenerative period.

By splitting your annual plan into identifiable phases and organis-ing these into cycles, all elements of your training plan will knit together. If organised correctly, they will allow you to be at your peak at a pre-determined time – something known as periodisation, which is an approach used by most serious or competitive swimmers.

Detraining and retraining

Training suggests systematisation, structure and orderliness. But what happens when a regular swimmer stops training? Quite simply, the swimmer will go into a phase known as 'detraining'. This detraining effectively means the loss of fitness gains, reversing the training process towards untrained levels. In order to move back towards the fully trained state, the swimmer will need to go through a process commonly known as 'retraining'.

'Swimming is the only form of exercise I take. I find other sports too exacting because they are all weight bearing.'

Helen Bown

Avoiding injury

Swimming is one of the safest of sports for people undergoing a fitness programme. Body weight is carried by the water during swimming, making the sport less taxing on joints and placing less stress on the skeletal structure during exercise. Many of the injuries that occur in other activities, particularly contact sports, very rarely occur in swimming. This makes it a great sport for those who either do not have the time to train regularly, or who are not very sporty in general. Swimming should, however, be treated with respect, and care needs to be taken to avoid some of the common pitfalls.

Swimming-related injuries and illnesses can be split into three types:

- Injuries that occur as a result of accidents on the poolside, e.g. slipping, or as a result of someone else swimming into you. Use your common sense to prevent these: take care when walking to and from the pool; avoid pools and swimmers with poor lane discipline; do not dive into shallow water; take a look before pushing off from the wall.

- Injuries that occur as a result of the swimming action itself, i.e. repetitive strain injuries. Be mindful of niggling pains. A small amount of pain while training is often something to be overcome, but regular and persistent pain in one area, inflammation or continuous soreness will tell you that this is something you cannot just swim off and needs rest – or even treatment by a physiotherapist.

- Illnesses and infections that are directly attributable to being in swimming pools or taking part in swimming as an exercise. Follow the basic hygiene and common sense guidelines given

'Swimming clears the mind, gives me an enormous sense of well-being and works every muscle in my body so I feel like I've had a good workout. It also doesn't place too much strain on any part of your body at one time, so is a great sport for those suffering from back or knee problems and sports injuries.'

Jo Head

below. If you are unwell, consult your GP – there are clearly certain occasions when persisting with your training programme will do you more harm than good. Swimming with a cold or flu is to be avoided, since you may make things worse and are likely to pass on your illness to others.

Basic swimming hygiene and good practice

Swimming pools with their warm, damp atmospheres are opportunities for germs and viruses to spread. In order to care for yourself, and in consideration of other bathers, follow the basic hygiene rules recommended by your pool. It's always best to try to avoid injury and illness in the first place. Take the following precautions:

- Have a warm shower before going into and after coming out of the pool, and walk through the footbath.
- Wash your hair if you have sufficient time on leaving to rinse out pool chemicals. If left in, these can damage your hair and cause minor skin irritation.
- Dry yourself thoroughly before leaving the pool (and avoid using someone else's towel). The temptation is to skimp on this when you are in a hurry, but dampness can encourage the development of fungal infections and skin irritations. In particular, dry inside your ears, your feet and between your toes after every session.
- Wrap up warm on cold days when leaving the pool.
- If you have long hair or find that your hair gets in the way when you are swimming, wear a swim cap. This will also prevent it from getting tangled in pool equipment etc.
- If you find that your eyes become sore during swimming, then lightweight goggles will make life easier.

Here we look at some of the common illnesses and injuries that can occur as a direct or indirect result of swimming, and at ways in which they may be prevented or alleviated. If you have any doubts with regard to illnesses or any form of injury, please consult your GP for advice.

Some common swimming-related ailments

Breaststroker's knee and chondromalacia patellae

Breaststroker's knee is one of the most common swimming ailments. If you consider breaststroke to be your best stroke, and swim it regularly, you are likely to have suffered some soreness from time to time. Pain is felt around the inside area of the knee due to excess strain of the medial ligament. Repeated bending of the knee and load-bearing while rotating the knee joint are the main causes of the soreness. This condition can be improved by narrowing the leg kick so that rotational strain on the medial ligament is reduced. Also, strengthening the quadricep muscles can help. Sometimes breaststroker's knee develops as a result not just of swimming breaststroke, but also of overloading the knee during land conditioning.

Chondromalacia patellae refers to damage to the under surface of the patella or softening of the knee cartilage. Pain can also be felt when the patella is pressed against the lower part of the femur upon extension of the knee and especially when climbing. This tends to cause creaking, grinding or crepitus. The collateral ligaments that lie around the knee inflame. Often, this condition – in which the pain is centred on the patella – occurs in tandem with a weak quadriceps muscle. If you do feel the onset of pain, you need to rest the knee. When pain has reduced, quadricep and hamstring exercises should be performed.

Eye irritation

The human eye easily becomes inflamed when it is subjected to pool water. The main cause of inflammation is the mix of human urea with that of water disinfectants. When the pH (acid-alkaline relationship) of water is significantly greater or lower than 7.4, pool water is more likely to cause eye irritation. Modern disinfectants tend to be less painful for the eyes.

Eye irritation becomes further exacerbated when the water is very warm and strong sunlight shines through so that the conjunctiva is also irritated. The eye really does become inflamed, with the cornea filling with water and resultant swelling. The tendency is then to rub the cornea and cause pink or red eye. Although a number of people still prefer to swim without goggles, these can all but eliminate eye irritation. You can even obtain goggles that are tinted to counteract strong sunlight when swimming. However, always use your own goggles to avoid contracting an infection from another swimmer.

Conjunctivitis can be highly contagious but is rarely serious and normally clears up after a few days. It is often an allergic reaction that produces tears, itching and a runny nose. If you simply cannot swim with goggles, eye-drops will help to relieve the condition; alternatively, try using a cold compress on your closed eye. If symptoms persist please consult your GP.

Ear and sinus infections

Obviously, your ears are in close contact with the water throughout swimming. Repeated movements in and out of the water can make it difficult to balance the air pressure inside the nose and ears with the water pressure outside. This can cause irritation in the sinuses and ears. Some people use nose-clips to help prevent this; others wear moulded earplugs (see also Chapter 2).

The most common ear infection among swimmers is known as *otitis externa*. If you don't dry your ears properly after training, water remains inside the ear canal and the moist warm conditions are perfect for bacterial growth. Further swimming, with its repeated movements in and out of the water, usually makes matters worse, and you may have to rest completely to rid yourself of the problem. So, if you suffer regularly from ear infections or inflammations it is particularly important that you dry inside your ears thoroughly at the end of each session. If you get an infection which persists, consult your doctor.

Ear infections are often related to nose and throat conditions. If you have a sinus infection, you may contract a middle ear infection because blowing your nose forces catarrh and pus up the Eustachian tube into the middle ear. Fluid then builds up behind the eardrum, causing a condition known as *serous otis media*. Antibiotics are usually needed in such cases. For this reason, it's best to avoid swimming until your condition has eased.

Infections of the feet

Athletes' foot (*tinca pedis*) occurs commonly among regular swimmers. If you don't dry the skin of your feet and between your toes properly, a fungal condition can develop which manifests itself as itchy blisters, especially between the toes. If the condition goes untreated it develops into cracked and blistered skin that can become infected. The fungi that cause it are part of a group called dermatophytes; they particularly like hot and damp atmospheres and feed on keratin, a protein found in nails and skin.

So how can you prevent and treat this irritant? Buy an over-the-counter anti-fungal ointment. Change your socks daily and ensure that your feet are dry at the end of swimming. Another way of reducing the infection is to soak your feet at home in warm, soapy water and then dry thoroughly. Also, avoid breaking off flaking skin; this can tear the healthy skin that is adjacent, thereby increasing the risk of spreading the infection.

Verruccas are another common and equally painful condition affecting the soles of the feet. They are caused by a virus similar to the one that causes warts on the hands. No treatment is required unless they become painful, as the body develops antibodies to the virus so that it can disappear on its own. However, if the verrucas do become painful, your doctor can treat the condition.

Problems with your hair

Unless you are careful, regular training can lead to a deterioration in the condition of your hair, causing split ends and bleaching (from strong sunlight reflected by the water). The use of a swim cap can help, but the best approach is to wash your hair immediately after swimming in order to get rid of any pool chemicals. Try not to get the shower water and shampoo into your ears while doing so! Use a conditioner on a regular basis if your hair needs it.

Anaemia

Iron-deficiency anaemia affects both men and women but tends to affect women more. Anaemia occurs when there is a reduced haemoglobin content in the red blood cells. Since these cells are responsible for transporting oxygen around the body to the exercising muscles in the form of oxyhaemaglobin, anaemia can adversely affect your ability to train as well as your general state of health – causing pallor, lethargy and excessive fatigue.

The recommended daily intake of iron is 12 mg for men and 14.8 mg for women. A normal diet contains 6 mg for every 1000 calories, so it follows that if you are consuming 3000–4000 calories each day, you should be meeting your iron needs. Always try to include foods that are rich in iron in your diet, such as dark green, leafy vegetables – spinach and watercress are especially good – pulses, red meat and eggs. This is particularly important for women who are training heavily, are pregnant, or who menstruate heavily. If you suspect that you are at risk of anaemia – or if you are experiencing unusual tiredness, breathlessness or light-headedness – consult your doctor. He or she will advise you whether or not you should be supplementing your iron intake.

'I'm pregnant at the moment and go swimming two or three times a week. The last time I was pregnant I swam until a late stage of my pregnancy and found it very helpful, as it was both relaxing and a weight-bearing exercise.'

Susie Carr

Tendinitis

One of the biggest single problems for swimmers is tendinitis, especially in the shoulder region (supraspinatus tendinitis), caused by the repeated arm movements of the swimming stroke. While tendinitis normally occurs in freestyle and butterfly, it also can be seen in backstroke where it takes the form of backstroker's shoulder. Here, the adduction and rotation movements of the arm when the hand is driven down into the water prior to the pull cause acute pain.

Tendinitis first of all affects the top of the shoulders. It becomes painful to lift the arms in any direction, but is more marked when lifting the arms laterally from the side of the body when in the standing position. This condition, which is sometimes known as frozen shoulder, makes it increasingly difficult to lift the arm above the head. If you are unfortunate enough to suffer from tendinitis, you may find that you get it when swimming one particular stroke. A change of stroke for a week can keep you in the swim and reduce the pain considerably. Ice packs applied to the area for a period of up to 20 minutes after a training session can further help to lessen the pain, although you will need a helpful pool staff to store the ice in a fridge for you while you swim. In general, strength and flexibility work can help to make you less susceptible to this condition (see pages 68–85 on land conditioning). You may also wish to check your stroke technique and correct any irregularities that may be causing the pain.

For some swimmers, the pain becomes acute and persistent. In such cases stop training and consult a medical practitioner.

Overtraining

Overtraining is when you train too much and your body does not have time to recover adequately between sessions, failing to adapt to the demands being made of it. This can be for a variety of reasons:

- the volume of swimming is too great or intense
- there is not enough rest between sessions, sets or swims
- the swimmer has unrealistically high personal goals
- there is too high an expectancy among family, friends or training partners.

If this happens, it is very easy to ease back before any damage is done. Often, though, you do not realise that your body has failed to adapt until is it actually happening. You therefore need to be aware of the symptoms, which include:

- an elevated resting heart rate (RHR) – by as much as 5 bpm
- listlessness and recurrent infections due to less efficient immune system
- poor training performance, e.g. your timed swims are slower
- difficulty in concentrating at work.

Be aware of your body, ensure that you have adequate amounts of carbohydrates and fluids in your diet (see Chapter 5), and plan your fitness programme carefully so that it is progressive and cyclical.

4 Training programmes

Types of training

Swimming training can be split into three types:

- long, continuous swims
- repetition or interval swims
- short, explosive swims.

All training programmes are written around these three main elements.

The long swims are further split into two areas: fartlek or 'speed play', and locomotive swimming. Fartlek normally involves swimming over longer distances at varying speeds, although the whole swim should never be exhausting. With locomotive training, the swimmer alternates fast and slow efforts but in a gradual way, e.g. 25 m slow, 25 m fast, 50 m slow, 50 m fast, 75 m slow, 75 m fast, 100 m slow, 100 m fast and so on. This type of swimming can include any ratio of lengths using the same format. Interval swimming is another term for repetition swimming, and involves taking a break between the allocated lengths. Short, explosive swims address anaerobic work.

Developing swimming endurance

Endurance is a key component of swimming fitness. Speed often comes after a base of endurance has been established. Generally, the best way to develop stamina for swimming is through swimming training itself.

Endurance training can be divided into four main areas:

Easy to moderate swimming

Aerobic swimming undertaken at an easy to moderate pace, i.e. 50–60 per cent of maximum heart rate (MHR), is suitable for anyone easing into a swimming training programme. You should be slightly breathless at the end of each of these swims but still be able to talk. During your re-introduction to a swimming programme, all your swimming should be done at this level. Later, when you are fitter, you will use such swimming for warm-ups and swim-downs (see also Chapter 3). Long, steady swims aiming for a heart rate of 130–140 bpm help the body to burn off fat through a process called lipid metabolism.

> '**I prefer pools that offer an adult fitness lane throughout the day. My work schedule means I can't be certain when I will get to the pool.**'
>
> *Sam Watkins*

Moderate to high-intensity swimming

Working at 70–80 per cent of your MHR is still primarily endurance work. You will find that your body can remove the lactic acid as you swim and so should not be totally exhausted. When you gain a reasonable level of swimming fitness you should aim for 70 per cent of your training to be done at this level.

High-intensity aerobic training

This is performed at 80–90 per cent of your MHR, and should be avoided if you have any conditions likely to be affected by this level of intensity and also for the first three to four months of your programme – although you should eventually aim to devote 10 per cent of your training to this level. Your efforts will be such that you are out of breath, your arms ache when you pull and you need a reasonable rest to recover from each repetition or swim that you make. Most swimmers try to introduce this type of training towards the back end of their sessions.

Anaerobic swimming

This refers to efforts made at a much more intense level, more than 90 per cent of your MHR. Basically, you are sprinting; pain increases as lactic acid builds in your muscles and oxygen debt sets in. If you are swimming at this level, you will need to take increasingly long rests between repetitions.

Repetition or interval swimming

Once you have begun swimming regularly again and have improved your level of swimming fitness, there are various types of repetition swims that you can try.

Interval swimming – referred to also as controlled interval swimming (CIS) – first came into the sport via athletics. It requires the swimmer to complete a sub-maximal set number of swims, all of the same distance, with the swim and rest amounting to the same amount of time for each repetition. The amount of rest you take is therefore predicated on the amount of time your repetition took. For example, if you were swimming 6 repetitions of 100 m freestyle on 2 minutes, your first swim might take 1 minute 35 seconds, leaving you with a 25-second rest. Your second swim could take 1 minute 25 seconds, leaving you a 35-second rest, and so on. These swims can be grouped to fit in with the energy systems discussed above. In other words, four swims of 100 m with 10 seconds rest will address aerobic conditioning because they would be performed at a lower intensity, while four swims with 2 minutes rest will clearly involve greater speed and physical intensity, thereby addressing anaerobic conditioning.

Terminology

CIS is normally expressed as swims being made 'off', 'at' or 'every' period of time. For example, four swims of 100 m aiming at a longer rest would be '4 × 100 m off 3½ min', while four swims aiming at a shorter rest would be '4 × 100 m off 2 min'. This would clearly depend on each individual's speed and the stroke involved.

Negative splits

Here, you swim the second part of your repetition faster than the first. Negative splits – or 'bringing things back harder' in coaching parlance – can be used for any type of repetition, not just CIS, and are a good way of teaching yourself pace and encouraging a balanced swim in terms of speed.

Broken swims

These are quite different from CIS. The swimmer completes a set number of repetitions but takes an extra and consistent break in order to let the heart rate drop slightly. If we take the example of (4 × 100 m off 3½ min), each of the 100 m swims would be further broken by a rest at 50 m. Broken swims are often made over slightly longer distances, although the breaks should be kept consistent throughout the repetitions – both in terms of the length of the rest and the point at which it is taken. Broken swims work particularly well if you are training seriously to take part in a Masters competition. During the tapering phase (i.e. the phase when you are easing back for competition – see p 112–13), they help to sharpen up pace and improve times. This is both a physical and a psychological benefit.

Alternating swims

Alternating swims are a way of breaking up the training to make it more interesting. The swimmer alternates two completely different types of swims: for example, 5 × 200 m freestyle alternating with 5 × 100 m breaststroke.

Mixed swims

These are a further way of adding variety to your sessions. For example, you might be swimming 4 × 200 m freestyle off 4 min. After the second 200 m repetition, you could add in 6 × 25 m breaststroke off 1 min.

Over-distance swimming

This consists of a small number of long repetitions at a medium to slow pace. The idea is to concentrate on technique and build a base level of cardiovascular fitness.

Standard rest swims

Not all repetition swims have to be made so as to integrate the time of the swim and the rest into a controlled interval. You could also take a standard rest between each swim – for example, 4 x 100 m freestyle with 10 seconds rest.

Breath control swims

The aim of breath-holding swims, sometimes also known as hypoxic training, is to teach you how to make better use of the available air. To do this, you simply take fewer breaths per length than normal, although as a training technique it is only relevant to freestyle. The lungs are very elastic and can take in a considerable amount of oxygen, but often very little of this is used. Improving oxygen uptake through training will in turn delay the onset of oxygen debt and so enable you to swim for longer before fatigue sets in.

This form of training puts the body under pressure by asking it to work without sufficient oxygen. The aim is to create more red blood cells to aid the absorption of oxygen from the lungs and improve cardiovascular efficiency. Not only does it build breath control, it is also useful for those who want to race since it will teach you to keep your head to the front as well as down at the end of the event.

Here is how you might go about your hypoxic swimming. Swim 200 m freestyle. For the first 50 m, breathe every arm cycle; for the second 50 m, breathe every second arm cycle; and so on until you reach four arm cycles (8 arm pulls). This is probably the maximum you want to do until you get used to this system of swimming. After a bit of practice, you will be able to work on even longer arm cycles to each breath.

'Front crawl is my favourite stroke. I find it the best way of clocking up distance during a short lunchtime break.'

Claire Kerslake

High-quality sets

These are also known as fast interval sets and are designed to put the swimmer under maximum pressure. They feature longer rests but your efforts are made at maximum speed – normally somewhere between 8 and 12 per cent slower than your best time for that distance. You would normally start the set with time targets in mind. These types of swims are useful for building up speed and working the fast-twitch muscle fibres that are responsible for sprinting. High-quality sets very quickly deplete body reserves, and too much of this type of training before you compete can be debilitating. There is therefore a fine line between these sets being beneficial and detrimental to your fitness training. You will need to work towards high-quality sets over a period of time by first working on swims that are less tiring.

Descending or reducing repetitions

These repetitions are very popular with competitive swimmers, as they provide a focus on continuous improvement. The swimmer follows the pattern of CIS but aims to swim progressively faster for each repetition.

Regressive repetitions

With regressive swims, you make your fastest effort first and your slowest last, but they are rarely used. You may, however, want to introduce them into your training programme to help create levels of speed awareness.

Measuring your performance using your heart rate

Measuring your heart rate after each repetition is a useful guide to how you are progressing. For example, if you replicate a set of swims made in a previous swimming session and find your heart rate has dropped, you are likely to be on the right track.

Here is a simple way of measuring your performance. We will take a set of swims, for example, 5 × 200 m backstroke off 4½ min. There is a reasonable amount of rest and the swims are of moderate intensity. Using an HRM, try to maintain a heart rate of 140 bpm. See how fast you can go for each 200 m effort while still maintaining that same heart rate. With each swim, try to go a little faster while keeping your heart rate in the range of 135 to 145 bpm.

The key to achieving this is by really focusing on your stroke efficiency – counting your strokes and attempting to reduce the number that you take for each length. Go back to your very first initiatives when starting your swimming programme. Concentrate hard on lengthening your push-off from the wall, making it as efficient as possible, and work on your breathing too.

Creating the right programme for you

Planning any training programme is really a decision-making process. After your initial couple of weeks of swimming you are faced with the first real decision – basically, whether to build your swims into an annual programme, or just to swim occasionally. On the assumption that you do decide to swim regularly throughout the year, you then need to decide on the following parameters before developing your programme:

- Are you going to train regularly but keep the training fairly light, or are you going to work towards a specific goal, perhaps a race or competition?
- Taking this decision into account, how many sessions do you plan to do each week?
- Then, how much time can you afford to give to each training session?
- And finally, what time of the day can you swim at? This question is important, as you will have to marry up the time that you can actually swim with work, social and family pressures – as well as with the times at which your local pool is available. Pools are often clearer during early-morning sessions, and some people prefer to swim at that time to start off the day in the right way. The disadvantages of this are having to get changed for work and possible fatigue making it hard to work afterwards.

Bear in mind that you do need to undertake a minimum amount of exercise to see fitness gains. The recommended exercise requirements for improving cardiovascular fitness are as follows:

Exercise requirements for improving cardiovascular fitness

Frequency	3–5 times a week, ideally varying the activities performed and altering the impact (and similarity of movement) in order to avoid repetitive strain or injury to joints and muscles.
Intensity	Working hard enough to cause the heart rate to increase to between 55 and 90 per cent of its maximum. Lower levels of intensity are appropriate for less active people.
Duration	Between 15 and 60 minutes is an optimal length of time, with approximately 30 minutes being sufficient to maintain any given fitness level. Less fit individuals need to progress gradually to this duration.

Activities that use the large muscle groups, require oxygen and are rhythmic in cadence are most effective. Most people, unless they are retired, can only afford to give up about an hour per session two or three times a week. Given today's busy lifestyles, few of us can swim every day – however much we would like to. This obviously limits the distance you will be able to cover in a week.

As a guide, world-class 1500 m swimmers are capable of swimming at the rate of about 5000 m an hour – given that a world-class 1500 m time is approximately 15 minutes. If you are capable of working at 4000 m per hour, you will be working at a really hard rate with little rest and probably little variety in your training. On the other hand, the average swimmer, looking for plenty of variety in their training, should aim to cover 2500–3000 m per session. In a 25-m pool, this amounts to around 100 lengths. You need to allow some three months to build up to this level (see also pp. 64–7, on planning your swimming year).

Finally, you need to decide what your goal is for the year. Most people embark on a programme to get fit, but beyond that objective there is often a further goal, for example getting your body in shape, looking good or overcoming illness (for example, to improve your asthma) or an injury. The important thing is to keep that goal in the back of your mind throughout your training, so that you can maintain your motivation and answer the question 'why am I doing this?' Sometimes, when you are tired and you know that getting fitter is going to involve some discomfort as well as pleasure, it is hard to stay motivated.

The more serious swimmer will need a specific target, such as a race or competition, to aim for. Your training programme will need to be directed towards the race you have in mind: for example, if you are going to compete in a 400 m race at the end of the year, your training needs to be tailored to this rather than focusing on, say, sprint training (see also pp. 45–50 on different training methods). Therefore, start with your objective and work backwards in planning your programme.

'Kick-start' training programme

The first month is the hardest part: try not to be over-ambitious. At first, it is better to concentrate on technique and breathing, and easing your way back into regular swimming. Work out a basic structure for your first few weeks' training, such as that suggested in the table below.

Suggested framework for the first three months

Month	Week	No. of sessions	Length of session	Distance per session*
1	1	1	30 min	300 m
	2	1	30 min	400 m
	3	2	45 min	600 m
	4	2	45 min	750 m
2	1	2	45 min	800 m
	2	2	45 min	800 m
	3	2	1 hr	1200 m
	4	2	1 hr	1200 m
3	1	2	1 hr	1500 m
	2	2	1 hr	1500 m
	3	2	1 hr	2000 m
	4	2	1 hr	2000 m

*Not including warm-up/swim-down

The tables below give some suggestions for the content of your training sessions for the first three months.

Sample training session – month 1, week 2, session 1

Distance (m)	Stroke	Rest between repetitions	Concentrate on
50	Freestyle		Very loose, easy warm-up
4 x 50	Freestyle	1 min	Breathing out fully before inhaling
2 x 50	Backstroke legs	1 min	Straightening the legs on the upkick
50	Backstroke		Loosen-off

Total distance: 400 m

Sample training session – month 1, week 2, session 2

Distance (m)	Stroke	Rest between repetitions	Concentrate on
100	Backstroke		Very loose, easy warm-up
3 x 100	Freestyle	1 min	Stroke counting, trying to complete the pull right back to the hips
4 x 25	Breaststroke	30 sec	Pausing slightly with the arms stretched out in front at the end of each kick
100	Freestyle		Loosen-off – work on breathing out

Total distance: 600 m

Sample training session – month 1, week 4, session 1

Distance (m)	Stroke	Rest between repetitions	Concentrate on
100	Freestyle		Finishing off the pull at the hips
6 x 50	Freestyle-progressive	1 min	Timing yourself, aiming to swim faster each time. Start very slowly and make the last swim as fast as you can
10 x 25	Alternating freestyle and backstroke legs	30 sec	Working with your hands in front of you in the freestyle, concentrating on getting the lower legs high; do the backstroke with your hands on your thighs
100	Backstroke		Loosen-off

Total distance: 750 m

Sample training session – month 2, week 2, session 1

Distance (m)	Stroke	Rest between repetitions	Concentrate on
200	Freestyle – breathe every 4 strokes		Centring the head once in every arm-cycle
4 x 50	Freestyle legs with kick board	45 sec	Small kicks, emphasising the shaking of the ankles
14 x 25	Freestyle arms with pull buoy	45 sec	Keeping the elbows high and the fingers relaxed on recovery
200	Alternate backstroke and breaststroke		Loosen-off

Total distance: 800 m

Sample training session – month 3, week 1, session 1

Distance (m)	Stroke	Rest between repetitions	Concentrate on
200	Backstroke		Warm-up
6 x 75	Freestyle – 25 kick, 25 pull, 25 stroke	45 sec	Working on stroke lengthening by building through the arms only to the full stroke each time
4 x 100	Freestyle – bilateral	45 sec	Concentrating on breath control
3 x 100	Breaststroke	1 min	Trying to lift the heels high in the recovery phase
100	Freestyle		Relaxing the fingers during the arm recovery

Total distance: 1500 m

Sample training session – month 3, week 4, session 1

Distance (m)	Stroke	Rest between repetitions	Concentrate on
400	Freestyle		Warming up with a focus on exaggerated pull back
10 x 100	Freestyle	45 sec	Swimming the second half of the swim faster than the first
10 x 25	Backstroke arms with pull buoy	30 sec	Pushing towards feet at the end of the arm stroke
10 x 25	Backstroke legs	30 sec	Tucking the chin in and trying to prevent the water coming over your face
8 x 25	Backstroke	45 sec	Leading the arm recovery with the little fingers
400	Breaststroke		Warming down with a focus on stretching through the front part of the stroke

Total distance: 1500 m

You will have noted that most of the swimming in the above sessions takes the form of freestyle. Freestyle is a good stroke for conditioning and getting fit: being the fastest stroke, it lends itself to 'getting more lengths under your belt', thus improving the efficiency of the cardiovascular system. Initially, you should adapt your rests to suit your fitness level, but after 3–4 weeks you will be able to take a systematic and consistent break.

No matter what strokes you are swimming, it is important to have a technical point to concentrate on during a session. This gives you greater focus and leads to continuous improvement. After a short period of time, you will be able to plan your own sessions with both fitness and technical goals in mind.

Swimming programmes

Your fitness swimming year will hinge on your objectives. Start by determining your goals. Then, you can decide which of the two programme structures given in the following pages is most appropriate to what you want to achieve. These are based on whether you want to improve your fitness base or swim in competitions.

Programme 1

If you decide that Programme 1 is the most suitable, then you will not be competing against other swimmers. You will probably want to be both looking and swimming at your best for two holiday periods: in April/May around the Easter holiday period; and in July/August, around the summer holiday period. On both occasions you may be swimming outdoors, either abroad or in the UK, and you will want to look and feel trimmer and fitter.

Programme 2

Programme 2 is for competitive swimmers. As a rule, there are two peaks to the competitive year. One peak is the short-course season in October, and the other is the long-course season in June (see p. 109). Those looking to compete should aim to peak twice a season, probably for a period of two to three days at the most. During the rest of the season you will not be able to record times close to those peaks.

The younger you are, the more likely you are to be able to compete close to your target or best times. As you get a little older, it becomes increasingly difficult to compete at your best level every week.

The table below gives some examples of what your annual goal(s) might be, matching these to the programme that will best help you to achieve them.

Matching your objectives to the right programme

Objective	Programme
To become generally fitter	1
To improve or recover my health	1
To improve my swimming for other water sports	1
To improve the technique of all my strokes	1
To swim a certain distance each week throughout the year	1
To socialise and take part	1 or 2
To become faster	1 or 2
To turn over a new leaf	1 or 2
To improve my swimming to help my triathlon, biathlon or pentathlon	1 or 2
To beat a specific time target during the year	1 or 2
To be the best for my age	2
To repeat the times achieved when previously a competitor	2
To race against friends or others	2
To complete an open-water swim of a certain distance	2

Your programme on a monthly basis

A goal-orientated approach to your planning will help you think ahead about your programme. You should know exactly what sort of training you should be undertaking during any month of the year in order to target it accordingly. This does not necessarily mean that you will know in advance what you plan to achieve in any one swimming session – or, for that matter, in any one week – but you should have an outline plan in your head. In other words, you start with your goal and work backwards.

There are considerable differences between what the fitness swimmer and the competitive swimmer need to achieve in their training programmes in order to reach their peaks. These are outlined in the month-by-month chart given below.

Differences in emphasis between the fitness programme (1) and competitive programme (2)

Month	Programme 1 emphasis	Programme 2 emphasis
September	Easy: peak condition first 2 weeks, then move back to medium swimming at end of month	Hard swimming
October	Medium swimming	Taper and race
November	Hard swimming	Hard swimming
December	Hard swimming	Hard swimming
January	Hard swimming	Hard swimming
February	Hard swimming	Hard swimming
March	Starting to ease up	Hard swimming
April	Easy swimming: concentrate on peak condition	Hard swimming
May	Easy swimming	Taper
June	Hard swimming	Taper and race
July	Hard swimming	Stay in race condition with medium swimming
August	Ease back: concentrate on peak condition	Begin to return to hard swimming

This can then be broken down into a general month-by-month analysis of your training content, as shown in the tables on the following pages.

Programme 1: fitness swimmers

Period and month	Training in pool	Body conditioning and planning
Preparation period Sept–Oct	■ Break into training steadily and build up to hard swimming in October ■ Work on swims of 200 m and 400 m with short rest ■ Work on kicking and pulling sets ■ If possible, video technique and play back ■ Monitor heart rates and record times swum as well as stroke-counting ■ Develop range of strokes ■ Get partner to help you with your technique	■ Start with a little distance running for general conditioning ■ Introduce endurance weights, i.e. high number of repetitions, low weight ■ Measure pulse rates when resting and exercising on land ■ Compare to rates in water ■ Lay down personal target training distances/times for season ■ Work hard on flexibility exercises or try yoga
Conditioning period Nov–Mar	■ Introduce starts and turns training. Work on your own initially ■ Increase quality of swims by going for faster times: work on pace ■ Maintain endurance base, i.e. aerobic work, but increase distances to 400 m and 800 m ■ Introduce more stroke drills ■ Continue to work on stroke technique with partner ■ Try kicking with fins and using hand paddles to increase resistance	■ Increase flexibility levels. Work with partner on flexibility ■ Test levels of flexibility to look for gains ■ Introduce heavier weights. Supplement free weights with use of fixed weights system ■ Keep regular check on weight and diet

Holiday period – peak fitness phase April	■ Swim much less. Work on high quality and reducing/descending swims (see also p. 50) ■ Bring in more swims of 50 m and 100 m with longer rests ■ Kick 50s to sharpen legs ■ Concentrate on quality of starts and turns	■ Decrease weights but maintain power work on legs ■ Increase flexibility work to reduce any stiffness emanating from weight programme ■ Be positive in your approach. Review achievements so far. Compare performances to goals. Reset goals
Return to conditioning phase May–July	■ Replenish lost endurance. Work on fartlek and over-distance training. 400–800 m swims, add freestyle breathing exercises ■ Increase variety by adding strokes, CIS etc. ■ Work on reducing sets but over longer distances; decrease rests	■ Keep strength training at similar levels while you increase distance training loads in water ■ Get partner to help refine weights technique ■ Maintain flexiblity
Holiday period –second peak phase Aug	As per April	As per April

Programme 2: competitive swimmers

Period and month	Training in pool	Body conditioning
Conditioning/ preparation period Nov–Feb	▪ Break into training steadily and build up to hard swimming ▪ Work on swims of 400 m and 800 m with short rest ▪ Get partner to help you with your technique ▪ Work on kicking and pulling sets ▪ If possible, video technique and play back ▪ Monitor heart rates and record times swum as well as stroke-counting ▪ Develop range of strokes	▪ Start with a little distance running for general conditioning ▪ At the beginning, start with endurance weights, i.e. high number of repetitions, low weight ▪ After a month, introduce heavier weights, going for power with fewer repetitions ▪ Measure pulse rates when resting and exercising on land. Compare to rates in water ▪ Lay down target times for season ▪ Work hard on flexibility exercises or try yoga
Pre-competitive/ step-up period Mar–May	▪ Introduce starts and turns training ▪ Increase quality of swims by going for faster times: train and work on pace ▪ Maintain endurance base, i.e. aerobic work over 400 m and 800 m while increasing quality and introducing swims of 150–200 m ▪ Introduce more stroke drills ▪ Continue to work on stroke technique with partner ▪ Try kicking with fins or pumps, swimming in a T–shirt and using hand paddles to increase resistance	▪ Increase both flexibility and strength training levels. Work with partner on flexibility ▪ Test levels of flexibility to look for gains ▪ Supplement free weights with use of fixed weights system ▪ Keep regular check on weight and diet. Sleep regular and consistent hours

Long-course competitive phase June	Work on high quality and reducing/descending swims (see p. 50) Bring in more 50s and 100s with longer rests Kick 50s to sharpen legs Retain some endurance with some longer aerobic swims over 400 m without too much overload Concentrate on quality of starts and turns Work on broken swims over competition distance	Decrease weights but maintain power work on legs Increase flexibility work to reduce any stiffness resulting from weights programme Prepare mind for competition by race planning Be positive in your approach. Review achievements so far. Compare performances to goals. Reset goals
Mid-season July–Sept	Replenish lost endurance. Work on fartlek and over-distance training. 400–800 m swims, add freestyle breathing exercises Increase variety by adding strokes, CIS etc. Work on reducing sets but over longer distance; decrease rests	Keep strength training at similar levels while you increase distance training loads in water Get partner to help refine weights technique Maintain flexibility
Short course competitive phase October	As per June	As per June

The next stage is to work out what you are actually doing in your individual training sessions.

The schedules

Following are some swimming schedules to get you started. They are based on a sample workout for each month of the year, for both fitness and Masters swimmers.

Key:

Individual medley – consists of butterfly, backstroke, breaststroke and one stroke not of the first three, in that order

@/off – the time taken for the swim + rest

+ (a time) – the amount of time to be taken for the rest

1st/2nd choice – your preferred or second-choice stroke

Sample workout for each month of the year by content and distance

Fitness swimmer		Competitive swimmer	
Content	Distance (m)	Content	Distance (m)
September		**September**	
■ 200 easy backstroke warm-up	200	■ 400 backstroke warm-up: concentrate on deep arm position on hand entry	400
■ 10 x 100 @ 2 min 1st choice	1000		
■ 6 x 50 kick + 10 sec backstroke legs	300	■ 8 x 200 @ 4 min – 1st choice: broken @ 100 by 10 sec – negative splits	1600
■ 400 freestyle stroke-counting	400	■ 12 x 50 + 30 freestyle legs	600
■ 6 x 50 arms + 10 sec: 1st choice with pull buoy	300	■ 10 x 50 reducing, sprints @ 2 min 30, 2nd choice	500
■ 100 ease-down	100	■ 200 very floppy warm-down	200
Total	2300	Total	3300
October		**October**	
■ 300 alternating back-stroke/freestyle warm-up	300	■ 600 freestyle – stroke-counting	600
■ 4 x 200 freestyle @ 3 min 30 sec	800	■ 8 x 100 1st choice @ 4 min – high quality	800
■ 6 x 75 + 15 sec alternating 1st/2nd choice	450	■ 200 easy freestyle	200
■ 8 x 50 + 10 sec breast-stroke legs with hands by side	400	■ 6 x (4 x 25) CIS + 30 sec	600
		■ 8 x 50 @ 2 min 30 sec, reducing freestyle	400
■ 400: 1st choice fartlek with loosen-down	400	■ 300 ease-off concentrating on breathing	300
Total	2350	Total	2900

November			
■ 8 x 50 + 5 sec 2nd choice warm-up	400	■ 400 alternating back-stroke/freestyle warm-up	400
■ 4 x 300 freestyle + 20 sec, reducing	1200	■ 6 x 200 freestyle @ 3 min 30 sec	1200
■ 5 x 100 + 10 sec alternating pull/kick on 3rd choice	500	■ 8 x 75 + 5 sec alternating 1st/2nd choice	600
■ 300 glide breaststroke, concentrating on getting the best out of the kick	300	■ 10 x 50 + 10 sec breast-stroke legs with hands by sides	500
■ 200 warm-down on freestyle	100	■ 400: 1st choice fartlek with loosen-down	400
Total	2500	Total	3100

December			
■ 200 bilateral freestyle	200	■ 10 x 50 + 5 sec 2nd choice warm-up	500
■ 4 x 200 alt. with 4 x 100 1st choice @ 3 min 30 and 2 min – testing heart rate	1200	■ 6 x 300 freestyle + 20 sec, reducing	1800
■ 6 x 50 + 10 breaststroke pull	300	■ 5 x 100 + 10 sec alternating pull/kick on 3rd choice	500
■ 600 backstroke alt. stroke/legs only	600	■ 300 glide breaststroke, concentrating on getting the best out of the kick	300
■ 6 x 50 + 10 breaststroke legs	300	■ 200 warm-down on freestyle	200
■ 200 freestyle loosen-down	200		
Total	2800	Total	3300

January			
■ 400 freestyle – normal breathing 1st length, breathe every 3 strokes on 2nd, every 4 strokes on 3rd and so on	400	■ 400 freestyle – normal breathing 1st length, breathe every 3 strokes on 2nd, every 4 strokes on 3rd and so on	400
■ 4 x 400 + 15 freestyle: descending – final target times 20 sec slower than personal best	1600	■ 5 x 400 + 15 freestyle: descending – final target times 20 sec slower than personal best	2000
■ 4 x 100 + 10 alt. 2nd/3rd choice legs	400	■ 6 x 100 + 10 alt. 2nd/3rd choice legs	600
■ 300 dive breaststroke – stroke drill	300	■ 300 dive breaststroke – stroke drill	300
■ 4 x 50 @ 1 min: 1st choice sprints	200	■ 4 x 50 @ 1 min: 1st choice sprints	200
Total	2900	Total	3500

Fitness swimmer		Competitive swimmer	
Content	Distance (m)	Content	Distance (m)
February			
■ 16 x 25 + 5: 2nd choice, warm-up concentrating on strong push-off	400	■ 200 easy backstroke warm-up	200
■ 3 x 600 + 15 freestyle – alt. steady and fast lengths	1800	■ 10 x 150 @ 2 min 30 sec 1st choice	1500
■ 8 x 25 + 5: backstroke legs	200	■ 8 x 50 kick + 10 sec backstroke legs	400
■ 300 freestyle catch-up – stroke drill	300	■ 600 freestyle stroke-counting	600
■ 6 x 25 + 15 butterfly fast	150	■ 8 x 100 arms + 10 sec: 1st choice wih pull buoy	800
		■ 100 ease down	100
Total	2850	Total	3600
March			
■ 300 backstroke warm-up: concentrate on deep arm position on hand entry	300	■ 400 bilateral freestyle	400
		■ 6 x 200 alt. with 6 x 100 1st choice @ 3 min 30 and 2 min – testing heart rate	1800
■ 6 x 200 @ 4 min – 1st choice: broken @ 100 by 10 sec – negative splits	1200	■ 6 x 50 + 10 breaststroke pull	300
■ 8 x 50 + 30 freestyle legs	400	■ 800 backstroke alt. stroke/legs only	800
■ 8 x 50 reducing, sprints @ 2 min 30, 2nd choice	400	■ 6 x 50 + 10 breaststroke legs	300
■ 200 very floppy warm-down	200	■ 200 freestyle loosen-down	200
Total	2500	Total	3800
April			
■ 400 freestyle – stroke-counting	400	■ 16 x 25 + 5: 2nd choice, warm-up, concentrating on strong push-off	400
■ 4 x 100 1st choice @ 4 min – high quality	400	■ 4 x 600 + 15 freestyle – alt. steady and fast lengths	2400
■ 200 easy freestyle	200		
■ 4 x (4 x 25) CIS + 30 sec	400	■ 12 x 25 + 5: backstroke legs	300
■ 8 x 50 @ 2 min 30 sec, reducing – freestyle	400	■ 400 freestyle catch-up – stroke drill	400
■ 300 ease-off concentrating on breathing	300	■ 6 x 50 + 15 butterfly fast	300
Total	2100	Total	3800

May

■ 4 x 100 individual medley	400
■ 4 x 300 + 10 freestyle: breathe every 4 strokes – negative splits	1200
■ 4 x 200 + 15, 2nd choice arms alt. with 4 x 100 1st choice legs	1200
■ 4 x 50 + 10 breaststroke	200
Total	**3000**

■ 2 x (4 x 100) individual medley	800
■ 4 x 300 + 10 freestyle: breathe every 4 strokes – negative splits	1200
■ 6 x 200 + 15, 2nd choice arms alt. with 6 x 100 1st choice legs	1800
■ 4 x 50 + 10 breaststroke	200
Total	**4000**

June

■ 200 alt. backstroke and freestyle	200
■ 2 x 800 + 15– each 800 broken into 200s:1st full stroke, 2nd arms only, 3rd legs only, 4th full stroke hard	1600
■ 4 x 50 + 5 butterfly legs	200
■ 4 x 50 + 5 butterfly legs swum with lateral kick	200
■ 4 x 50 + 5 butterfly	200
■ 4 x 50 + 5 backstroke legs	200
■ 4 x 50 + 5 backstroke legs with hands locked above head	200
■ 4 x 50 + 5 backstroke	200
Total	**3000**

■ 400 freestyle – stroke-counting	400
■ 4 x 150 + 1 min 30 – reducing, broken by 10 sec @ 75	600
■ 400 pull, kick, swim alt. length on freestyle	400
■ 4 x 75 + 2 min high quality – concentrate on explosive dive	300
■ Starts and turns practice: 10–15 min	
■ 4 x 25 + 1 min – 1st choice	100
■ 200 loosen-off	200
Total	**2000**

July

■ (4 x 100) reverse individual medley	400
■ 16 x 25 + 5: 2nd choice, hard kick	400
■ 4 x 400 + 10: 1st choice alt. steady/hard 100s within each 400	1600
■ 4 x 100 individual medley legs only – broken by 5 sec at 100s	400
■ 4 x 100 individual medley arms only – broken by 5 sec at 100s	400
■ 2 x (4 x 25) individual medley	200
Total	**3400**

■ 4 x 100 reverse individual medley	400
■ 8 x 25 + 45: 2nd choice, hard kick	200
■ 6 x 100 freestyle @ 3 min 30 sec: high quality	600
■ 200 glide breaststroke – fairly easy	200
■ 6 x 75 @ 2 min 30 sec: 1st choice – reducing	450
■ 200 loose backstroke	200
■ 6 x 25 @ 1 min 30 sec – 1st choice hard	150
Total	**2200**

Body conditioning exercises

A body conditioning programme can both support and enhance what you are doing in the water, and is advantageous for a variety of reasons:

- you may find it difficult to get to the pool on a regular basis, but have a gym nearby or can train at home;
- your colleagues or coach tell you that you are quite stiff in the water and hence some flexibility work would not go amiss;
- you know that you are not as strong in the water as you should be, and therefore a strength programme on land could help to increase power;
- you lack the motivation to constantly swim lengths to get fit, and so add land conditioning for variety.

Nearly all of the endurance required for swimming can be built up in the water, although running in the early part of the season can be beneficial. However, very little muscular strength can be gained by swimming alone, so body conditioning is a necessity for increased power. As far as flexibility is concerned, this is best developed in the water itself – the benefit of flexibility work on land lies in the extra resistance it can offer (see below).

Flexibility

Why should swimmers bother with flexibility work? Apart from its importance to your general health and comfort, the main reason is that it helps to increase the range of motion (ROM) of muscles and joints. As the range of limb movement increases, so the efficiency of the stroke is improved. In theory, the amount of drag should similarly be reduced because of the swimmer's ability to overcome resistance.

Broadly speaking, stretching can be either static or dynamic (moving). In static stretching, you take a part of the body to the point at which a stretch is felt. You then hold that position – usually for 15–30 seconds – during which time the muscle gradually relaxes. The stretch should be released slowly to allow a gradual release in tension. Always ensure that you are fully warmed up and in a comfortable position for this type of flexibility work: kneeling and single-leg standing should generally be avoided. Dynamic stretching involves movement, and so must be carried out gently and progressively to avoid injury: a good example is circling the arms, as described on pp. 22–23.

While stretching can be done on your own, it is sometimes more effective when carried out with the help of a training partner. Since your partner can encourage a greater stretch than you would be able to achieve alone, take great care with this kind of work, and always ensure that the person being stretched gives continuous feedback.

Whatever type of flexibility work you are doing, build up steadily and gradually increase the range of movement without pain. Some sample stretching exercises are given over the following pages and are intended to help you improve your flexibility over time. Please note that several exercises are for more advanced swimmers and should not be attempted unless or until you have built up your general programme and flexibility to a good base level.

Measuring your flexibility

When you start your training programme, it's useful to measure your flexibility so that you have a means of assessing any progress made – as a result of both swimming itself, and your land conditioning work. You can record the results in your training diary.

Shoulders

The ability to flex and extend your shoulders is paramount in all swimming strokes. In backstroke, for example, increased flexibility can help you drive your hands deeper into the water behind the head after the hand entrance and prior to the pull. The capacity to hyper-flex the shoulder is of value in increasing the range of movement in the pull. Here is a quick way of measuring your shoulder flexibility so that you can test yourself from time to time:

'I feel much better after an early morning swim. I'm much more alert at work and can concentrate more on what I'm doing.'

Janet Tanner

Shoulder flexion

Lie on the floor with your face to the ground and your arms extended above your head, hands locked together. Then, while keeping your chin on the floor and the fingers of your hands locked throughout, lift your

hands as high as they will go. Keep the movement slow and gentle. Get a partner to measure the distance between your hands and the ground: this is your baseline for the future, as you will look to increase the distance during your fitness programme.

Shoulder extension

This is another easy measurement. Stand up straight and stretch your hands back as shown here, keeping your arms as much in line with the shoulder as possible. Your partner then needs to measure the distance between your two hands.

Here are some exercises to aid shoulder flexibility.

- Hold a towel with both arms in front of you by your thighs. Keeping your arms straight, bring the towel in a controlled fashion through 180 degrees and over your head so that it comes to lie behind your buttocks. Then bring it back over your head to the starting position. Do this several times. Slowly, as you become more flexible, you will be able to move your hands closer together along the towel.

- Lying on a bench, get a partner to hold your elbow and wrist as you mimic a high elbow recovery on freestyle. Your partner then very gently pushes your elbow in towards the centre of your back. Hold the stretch for 15–30 seconds, then relax. Repeat on the other side.

- Lying on the floor face-down, place both hands in the small of your back. Your partner kneels at your head and takes hold of the outer part of your elbows. They then lean backwards, gently pulling your arms inwards and upwards. Hold the stretch for 15–30 seconds, relax and repeat.

- Stand, placing your left hand behind your head on your left shoulder blade. Press gently and steadily with your right hand on your left elbow, so as to move your left hand as far down your back as possible. Keep your back straight, your shoulders down and face forwards throughout. Hold for 15–30 seconds then relax. Repeat on the other side.

- To extend the previous exercise, place the palms of your hands behind your head and on opposite shoulder blades (effectively, the arms cross at the forearms). Gently stretch the fingers of both hands as far down your back as possible.

- Standing upright, with your arms out to the side in line with your shoulders, try to move your hands backwards using a series of small, controlled bounces. Then try the same exercise but with your arms straight up above your head.

- Finally, try single-arm circles through 360 degrees in both directions. Throughout the exercise, stand up straight and face forwards. Keep your arms close to your head, and don't let your shoulders lift. Repeat on both sides and in both directions. Then change to backward and forward circles with both arms – make the movements in this exercise a little slower so that the shoulders almost scrape together. Then, bend forwards slightly and copy butterfly arms movements, swinging the arms a little more vigorously.

Feet and ankles

Foot and ankle flexibility is essential for swimming. Flexibility in the ankles increases the extension of the feet, enabling a larger range of movement in all strokes – and particularly in backstroke and breaststroke, where the leg action plays an important part. In addition, this flexibility enhances the propeller-like movement so necessary to create lift force.

Here is a quick way of measuring your ankle flexibility so that you can test yourself from time to time. For all ankle measurements, you will need to carry out the following preliminaries. Take a large proctrator and an A3 piece of paper. Place the proctractor over the paper and mark in the degrees in pencil. Then stick the paper to a wall, so that it touches the floor.

Plantar flexion

Sit on the ground with your legs outstretched so that your feet are adjacent to the paper on the wall. Keeping your ankles together, point your toes and press them down towards the ground. Get a partner to measure the number of degrees through which your toes move – from a position where they are curled up towards the body to when they are pointing towards the ground.

Dorsi flexion

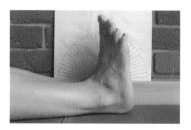

In the same position, start with your feet relaxed and hanging loosely. Then curl your toes up towards you as far as possible. Once again, ask your partner to measure the degree of movement achieved.

Eversion and inversion

Remove your paper from the wall and place it on the ground. Sit on the floor so that the heel of your foot is placed over the centre point of your protractor layout, i.e. at 90 degrees. Keeping your heel on the centre point and on the ground, stretch your big toe as far outwards as you can (eversion) and then as far inwards (inversion). For each movement, hold the position while a partner measures the angle your ankle makes to the protractor.

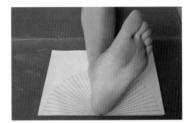 

Here are some exercises to aid ankle flexibility, all of which are static in nature.

- Sit with your legs outstretched and straight at the knees. Hook a towel over your toes and pull your toes towards your body. Hold for 15–30 seconds, relax and repeat.

- Stand on one leg and loop the towel over your raised foot. Pull the towel and the foot so that your sole is squeezed to your backside. Ensure that your knee is pointing downwards, your legs are pressed together, and avoid hollowing your back. Repeat on the other side.

- Kneel on the ground with your toes pointed rather than curled. Place a towel under your feet for cushioning. With your hands placed on the ground on either side of your shoulders to provide balance, and your chin forwards, carefully rock back, extending the toes.

- Sitting with your legs outstretched and straight, feet together, point your toes towards the ground. Then, rotate your feet so that your big toes face in to one another.

- Remaining in the same position, keep your heels on the ground and fan your feet outwards so that your little toes are 'trying' to meet the ground.

- Now stand with your heels together and your feet facing outwards. Bend your knees as shown, keeping your back straight and head up. Hold for 15–30 seconds then relax and repeat.

- Lie on your front with one elbow in front stabilising you in an upright position. Bend one leg up and reach to hold the toes of one foot in the crook of your elbow on the same side. Pull your foot gently towards the small of your back. Hold for 15–30 seconds then change feet. This exercise also stretches the quadriceps muscle at the front of the thigh.

- Standing, lean and reach forwards against a wall with your arms straight. The legs also stay straight. Keep the soles of your feet flat on the ground and gradually move your feet back so as to stretch the ankles and the calf muscles.

- Sit facing another swimmer with your legs slightly apart. Your partner holds the heel of your foot in one hand and the toes in the other, and gently presses your toes outwards towards the ground.

Trunk and hips

In swimming, reasonable flexibility of the trunk and hips is important for general body position – and flexibility of the hips aids hip rotation. There are no handy hints for measurement as there are for the shoulders, feet and ankles, but here are some useful exercises that you may wish to try.

- Sit on the ground with one leg outstretched. The other leg is bent, with the sole of the foot positioned against the inside of the outstretched leg. Bend forwards slowly from the hips, keeping your back straight, while reaching towards the foot of your outstretched leg. Hold for 15–30 seconds then relax. Repeat on the other side.

- Lie face-down on the ground. Hold your ankles with your toes pointed. Keeping your head up, gently rock backwards and forwards, pushing your hips downwards to achieve the stretch. (Take care if you have any problems with your back or neck.)

- Sit on the floor with your knees out and the soles of your feet together. Clasp your hands around your feet and gently pull downwards, aiming to place your forehead on your feet. Hold the stretch for 15–30 seconds, relax and repeat.

- Now lie on your front with your hands on the ground by your sides, fingers facing forwards. Keeping your feet on the floor, push upwards and slowly arch your back – first up on to your elbows and then, for a more intense stretch, up on to your hands. Hold for 15–30 seconds then relax. Follow this by placing your hands together behind your back and arching once again; then with your hands on either side of your head and your elbows back. Keep your feet firmly on the floor throughout.

As alternative forms of flexibility work, both Pilates and yoga – where breath control forms part of the programme – should be considered.

Strength training

While muscular endurance improves through swimming, strength is something that cannot easily be developed in the water. A weight training programme, supported by a diet rich in carbohydrate and protein (see also pp. 87–97) can help build muscle tissue and make your swimming more powerful. Again, if you have recently embarked on a training programme, build into the strength training part gradually. The best way of breaking yourself in is to concentrate initially on endurance-based work, i.e. more repetitions with a lighter weight, rather than power work (a small number of repetitions with a heavy weight). Gradually, you can change the balance between the two. The number of repetitions and weight lifted will determine the degree of endurance and strength benefits that you will receive. As a guide, at first you need to select weights that will allow you to perform between 10 and 20 repetitions fairly easily, and to spend the first three to four weeks on endurance-based weight training.

Weight training in general can be split into free and fixed weights. Fixed weights are normally found at sports centres and swimming pools, and are easier and safer to use. However, many people find it more convenient to carry out their strength training from home, and so tend to use free weights.

Which muscles?

When strength training for swimming you need to concentrate on two things:

- exercises that focus on the muscles or muscle groups used to propel your body through the water
- exercises that reflect the movements used in swimming.

Select about six or seven exercises for each session, including some aimed at your abdominals as well.

Which exercise, which stroke?

Stroke	Exercise	Benefits
Freestyle	Pullover; triceps press; bench press; row; wrist curls; shoulder press; lat pulldown	Arms
	Bent-over rowing; calf raise; jump quarter squats; leg press	Legs
Breaststroke	Triceps press; bench press; row; wrist curls	Arms
	Calf raise; jump quarter squats; leg press; adductor machine	Kick
Backstroke	Pullover; triceps press; wrist curl; sideways lat raise; lat pulldown	Arms
	Calf raise; jump quarter squats; leg press	Kick
Butterfly	Pullover; triceps press; bench press; wrist curls; shoulder press; lat pulldown	Arms
	Calf raise; jump quarter squat; leg press	Legs

Using weights – some basic guidelines

As far as technique is concerned, there are a few important, common-sense points to bear in mind:

■ always warm up with light exercise that raises the heart rate before going into any weights session

■ do not try to lift a weight which is clearly too heavy for you

■ build up steadily towards a weight through a series of sets of increasing weight

■ when lifting and lowering any weight, try to make the movements as steady as possible. Avoid jerky movements and any undue strain which will result if a heavy weight pulls muscles out of position too rapidly

■ breathe out on exertion, and never hold your breath

■ if you are using free weights remember to keep your head up and your back as straight as possible so that you don't arch it.

Swimming exercises

It is not possible here to prescribe a set of weight training exercises that simulate exactly the movements involved in a swimming stroke. The figures below are examples of only one common leg and arm exercise that are beneficial for a particular aspect of each stroke. Many of the exercises use free weights, but can be replicated using fixed weight machines in the gym (the leg extension, leg press, lat pulldown all require the availability of such machines).

Freestyle – arms

Triceps press

Starting position	Instructions
This exercise can be tried kneeling – on a mat or towel as illustrated – standing, or lying on the floor or bench with your knees bent to help protect your back. Gripping the bar with your hands about 12 inches apart, hold it straight over your head, elbows extended and palms forwards as shown.	Carefully lower the barbell by flexing the elbows. Keep your elbows up and still as you do so. Return to the starting position as you exhale, ensuring that your back does not arch as you do so.

Freestyle – legs

Calf raise

Starting position	Instructions
With your shoulders under the pads of the machine, stand on the block with your heels hanging off the edge. Your feet should be hip-width apart. If a calf raise machine is not available, use a step instead, as shown here.	Rise on to your toes, hold the position briefly then lower your heels back down again, as far as they can go without overstretching the calf muscles. Repeat, keeping your legs straight and lower back flat throughout.

Breaststroke – arms

Bench press

Starting position	Instructions
Lift a barbell or dumbbells to your thighs (remember to keep your back straight and your head up) and sit on a bench, with the bar resting on your lap. Lie flat on the bench as shown, and roll the bar towards your chest. Grip the bar with your hands just slightly wider than shoulder-width apart.	Push the weight straight up above your chest and then bend your elbows to slowly lower it again. As soon as the barbell reaches your chest, repeat the exercise, exhaling as you push the weight upwards.

Breaststroke – kick

Inner thigh raise – adductors

Starting position	Instructions
Lie on your side, with your head resting on your lower hand and upper arm resting on the floor for support. Bend your upper leg, resting it on the floor as illustrated, and exhale as you slowly lift the lower leg as high as you can.	Keep your abdominals pulled in tightly, your back straight and your foot flexed and parallel to the floor throughout. Do the required number of reps and repeat on the other side. Use ankle weights to increase the intensity of the movement, paying particular attention to your form if you do.

Backstroke – arms

Pullover

Starting position	Instructions
Lie on your back with your knees bent – either flat on the floor or using a bench (flat or inclined) – holding a barbell with your arms outstretched behind your head as shown. Make sure your lower back remains in contact with the floor or bench at all times.	Keeping your arms straight, lift the weight smoothly in an arc from behind your head down to your thighs. Return the weight to the starting position and repeat. This exercise can also be performed with dumbbells.

Backstroke – kick

Leg extension

Starting position	Instructions
Sit on the leg extension machine and hook your feet under the pads as shown. Ensure that your lower back and thighs are fully supported, and hold on to the side-bars (or side of the seat) for balance.	Slowly straighten your legs. When you reach the top of the movement, i.e. when your legs are fully straight, hold that position briefly and then lower the weight back down in a controlled fashion. You can also do this exercise one leg at a time – although obviously using a lighter weight.

Butterfly – arms

Lat pulldown

Starting position	Instructions
Sitting down at the lat pulldown machine, reach up and hold the bar with your hands slightly wider than shoulder-width apart. Your feet should be flat on the floor and hip-width apart.	Bend your elbows and smoothly pull the bar down in front of your neck. Hold that position before returning the bar to the starting position. Breathe out as you pull down, and hold your abdominal muscles tight so that you don't arch your back.

Butterfly – legs

Leg press	
Starting position	Instructions
Sit on the apparatus with your knees bent as shown, grasping the side-bars.	Push forwards with your feet on the plate to straighten your legs (but do not lock your knees). Keep the movement smooth throughout, exhaling as you press with your legs, and inhaling as your knees bend and you return under control to the starting position. Contract your abdominal muscles so that you do not arch your back.

5 Nutrition

So much is written about diet and healthy living these days that the surfeit of information can be thoroughly confusing. This chapter sets out some straightforward guidelines for you if you are exercising regularly or if you perhaps want to take part in Masters swimming competitions from time to time.

The cornerstones of good body maintenance are regular meals, not smoking and regular sleep. Food is your source of energy and once you start exercising regularly you will need more of it if you are to maintain your body weight and get the most out of your training sessions. In short, your daily calorific intake and output need to balance each other. Before you were exercising regularly, you probably needed between 2,000 and 3,000 calories a day (depending on your level of activity) in order to maintain your weight. Depending on how much swimming you are doing, the number of calories you need to remain at the same weight can be up to 25 per cent greater.

> 'I always try to get something to eat within an hour following my swim. The swim requires a lot of energy and it's important for me to quickly replenish my reserves afterwards.'
>
> *Jolyon Burgess*

A healthy diet

The components of food provide the fuel for all activity. Carbohydrate, fat, protein and alcohol are all capable of producing energy, the amounts per gram being as follows:

- carbohydrate – 4 kcal
- fat – 9 kcal
- protein – 4 kcal
- alcohol – 7 kcal.

Carbohydrate is stored as glycogen in the muscles and liver, fat is stored as body fat (or adipose tissue) all over the body – as is an excess of any food component not required by the body – and protein is what muscle and tissue are made from. All but alcohol can therefore be used to fuel your swimming as they can all be used directly by the muscles. However, protein is only really used as an energy source during very intense or prolonged training sessions when your glycogen stores begin to run out.

Carbohydrate

Carbohydrates therefore provide fuel for almost every type of activity and are particularly important to people taking part in exercise such as swimming. Most of the energy needed for muscular contraction comes from this source, with the remainder being supplied from your fat stores. If carbohydrate levels are not replenished after exercising, you may not be able to train as effectively as you would like at your next session. Allow this to happen over a period of time and chronic fatigue can set in, resulting in a loss of interest in training and poor performance.

A real effort therefore needs to be made to increase carbohydrate intake on a daily basis, especially before and after hard training, to maintain sufficient glycogen stores. For most athletes, including swimmers, an intake of around 5–10 g of carbohydrate for every kilogram bodyweight will maximise daily muscle glycogen recovery. Alternatively, aim to get a minimum of 60 per cent of your daily energy from carbohydrates.

Energy systems

The intensity at which you swim determines the method by which your body provides you with energy. If you are swimming at a very high intensity (i.e. working anaerobically, or without oxygen), carbohydrate will be your main source of energy. The glycogen stored in your muscles is broken down into glucose, which produces energy and lactic acid. As your stores of muscle glycogen are not endless, your reserves quickly become depleted, while the lactic acid gradually builds up. Thus, if swimming at top speed you quickly feel a heavy, burning sensation in your arms and legs and your pulling movements become weaker.

However, if you swim at a more moderate pace so that your body is working aerobically, i.e. with oxygen, energy can be generated from both glycogen and fat. Although it produces energy more slowly than when your body is working anaerobically, this kind of energy production can be sustained for much longer periods of time so it is the aerobic system that is used mainly when you are swimming for fitness.

Which are the best sources of carbohydrate?

The glycaemic index (GI) has been developed by scientists to identify the immediate effect of a particular source of carbohydrate on blood sugar levels. It provides a scale which ranks foods from 0 to 100, with 100 working most quickly. All foods are compared to a base food such as glucose. This provides a useful reference for how your body will respond to various foods and will help determine the most suitable food to consume before, during and after exercise or competition. To find out more about GI, you will need to refer to a detailed sports nutrition book (see further reading suggestions on p. 120).

The most important point to remember here is that the higher the GI rating, the more quickly the carbohydrate is absorbed from your small intestine into your blood stream, and the faster it can be used by the muscle cells. A low GI meal taken one to two hours before you go to the pool can help your swim by generating slow-release energy. This will help delay fatigue.

Low GI foods that can be eaten an hour before exercise include:

- dried apricots (1 small handful)
- pasta (1 medium bowl)
- porridge (1 medium bowl)
- low-fat yoghurt (2 x 150 g cartons)
- muesli (1 medium bowl).

Note: Each portion will provide 50 g of carbohydrate.

Higher GI foods should be eaten after your swimming session. They will replenish the glycogen stores in your muscles immediately.

High GI foods that should be eaten immediately after exercise include:

- breakfast cereals
- skimmed milk
- pancakes
- bread
- bagels
- isotonic sports drink (higher in sugar).

Note: Each portion will provide 75 g of carbohydrate.

Fat

If you have decided to go back to swimming to lose weight you may well ask the question: 'Why do I need fat? Isn't it something I should avoid in order to keep slim?' It is not quite this simple. The key is to ensure that you consume the correct amount and type of fat to ensure a healthy body and one that is better able to perform at its best.

Dietary fat

Many carbohydrate-based foods will also offer sufficient fat for the average diet, although the Department of Health (DoH) recommends that a maximum of 33–35 per cent of your daily calorie intake comes from fat. There are three types.

Saturated fats are not considered good for you and have been linked to heart disease because they contribute to increased cholesterol levels. The DoH recommends a saturated fatty acid intake of no more than 10 per cent of total calorie intake.

Foods that contain *saturated fats* include:

- butter
- lard
- cheese
- meat fat
- all foods processed using these fats, including biscuits, cakes and pastries.

Monounsaturated fats, on the other hand, have been shown to have the greatest health benefits, helping to reduce total cholesterol without affecting other cholesterol benefits. The DoH recommends a monounsaturated fatty acid intake of up to 12 per cent of total calorie intake.

Foods that contain *monounsaturated* fats include:

- oils including olive, rapeseed, groundnut, hazelnut, almond
- avocado
- olives
- nuts and seeds.

Polyunsaturated fats can be found in vegetable oils and oily fish, and can help lower cholesterol levels. They are also important because they include the so-called 'essential' fatty acids, which cannot be made by the body so have to come from food (or supplements). Aim to eat about 10 per cent of your total calorie intake as polyunsaturated fats.

In general, you should monitor your fat intake and eat the correct amounts of each type to ensure that you get the most out of your body. Try to use olive oil for cooking, remove the skin from meats such as chicken and turkey and, as a general rule, grill or boil rather then fry.

Body fat

There are two types of body fat: essential fat and storage fat. *Essential fat* is what your body actually requires to function properly, providing insulation, protection and cushioning against physical damage. In a healthy person it accounts for roughly 3 per cent of body weight and can be found at specific sites such as around the heart, kidneys and liver. Women also have sex-specific fat that is essential to hormone (oestrogen and progesterone) production, and this is found in the breasts and around the hips. It accounts for a further 5–9 per cent of body weight.

Storage fat is an important energy reserve and can be found in the cells under the skin (subcutaneous) and around the organs. This fat is used almost all the time during any aerobic activity (including sleeping and walking around) and is relied on more heavily during exercise.

As a general rule, men should have between 13 and 18 per cent body fat, and women between 18 and 25 per cent body fat.

Protein

Protein accounts for about 20 per cent of your total body weight and is found in every cell and tissue in your body, including your muscles, tendons, internal organs, skin, hair and nails. It is primarily a building material – essential for growing and repairing muscular tissue after training, for instance – but has many other functions too, and can be used as a source of energy if you swim at a high level of intensity and for long periods of time.

If you have decided to invest in training for competitive swimming this will indeed involve regular, intense and prolonged exercise in the pool combined with a well-structured strength training programme. However, even if you are just starting out on a swimming programme it is very important to ensure that protein plays a part in your diet, and if you are vegetarian it is even more important to ensure that you are eating enough. The recommended daily intake for people who participate in regular exercise or sport is 0.75 g/kg bodyweight/day. If you are doing regular endurance training you will need to increase this intake to between 1.2–1.4 g/kg bodyweight/day. However, your exact protein needs depend on the type, intensity and duration of your exercise and you should refer to a more detailed text or a nutritionist to decide what is right for you.

The following foods are good sources of protein and should be incorporated into your daily meal plans:

- meat and fish (beef, chicken, turkey, cod, mackerel, tuna)
- dairy products and eggs (cheese, cottage cheese, skimmed milk, yoghurt, fromage frais, eggs)
- nuts and seeds (peanuts, peanut butter, cashew nuts, walnuts, sunflower seeds, sesame seeds)
- pulses (baked beans, red lentils, red kidney beans, chick peas)
- soya products (soya milk, soya mince, tofu)
- Quorn products
- grains and cereals (wholemeal and white bread, boiled pasta, brown and white rice).

Fluids

Despite the fact that while swimming you are surrounded by water you will still sweat! This is an important point to remember. It is also extremely important that you remember to replace lost fluid. The following few paragraphs are intended to help you understand and prevent dehydration during your swimming training.

How much will I sweat and how can I replace lost fluid?

The main function of sweating is to keep your body temperature down. When you exercise, your muscles will produce a lot of extra heat (75 per cent of the energy you are using up is converted into heat and then lost). If you become too hot (over 38°C) your vital body functions are in danger of being damaged. So, it follows that the more you exercise, the more your body needs to sweat in order to cool down.

How much fluid you lose when exercising will also depend upon external factors such as the humidity of the environment you are exercising in and your own body chemistry. Swimming pools are often kept at a warm temperature and the general humidity is high so you may actually lose a substantial amount of fluid. You will know if you are suffering from dehydration if you notice any of the following symptoms:

- sluggishness
- a general sense of fatigue
- headaches
- loss of appetite
- feeling excessively hot
- light-headedness
- nausea.

Another simple test is to examine your urine. If it is light or clear in colour, you are probably drinking enough; if it is dark in colour, you need to drink more.

The easiest way to combat dehydration is by drinking water on a regular basis. If you are swimming regularly, you should try to take in 1.5–2 litres per day plus a further 500 ml about 2 hours before training and an additional 125–150 ml immediately before swimming. You should also drink 500 ml as soon as possible after exercise. It is too late when you feel thirsty: you should have already taken in the fluid by this point. Keep a bottle of water in your sports bag and place it at the side of the pool, reminding you to drink before and after your session. The importance of regular fluid intake in order to avoid dehydration cannot be overstressed. How can you keep a check on whether you are taking enough fluid? There is a simple way. Weigh yourself before and after training. If you find you have lost one kilogram in body weight, you will need to replace it with 1.5 litres of fluid drunk over a period of time. Do not drink the whole amount immediately after exercise! You can always weigh yourself again an hour later when you get to work or at home. If you find that you are still down on weight, take in further fluids until you have recovered the loss.

Regular swimmers also lose water through conduction into the water while training. If you swim outdoors in the heat, you will lose more fluid than swimming indoors in the winter, although even then you can still become dehydrated. Try to take in more water in order to compensate for these losses and make sure that at least some of this is around the time of your swimming session.

> 'Swimming for me is a relaxing, low-effort experience. At the same time, it provides me with an outlet for intensive exercise.'
>
> *Charlotte Evans*

Sports drinks are also useful if you are training at a high intensity or taking part in competition because they contain carbohydrates. To help improve endurance and performance you need to consume approximately 1 g carbohydrate/kg bodyweight prior to exercise. Taking in the equivalent amount through a sports drink is just as effective.

Vitamins and minerals

Our bodies are unable to make vitamins and minerals, so they must be supplied in our diets. They are required for growth, health and physical wellbeing and also contribute to our enzyme system – the system that enables all our metabolic functions – immune system, hormonal system and nervous system. Minerals are vital to regulatory and structural functions of the body.

If you eat a good balanced diet you should automatically achieve a high vitamin and mineral intake. However, regular, intense exercise increases your requirements for a number of essential vitamins and minerals, especially those involved in energy production, tissue growth and repair and blood levels. Those of particular importance are listed in the table overleaf. A balance of vitamins is important. A deficiency in vitamins B and C, the water-soluble vitamins, leads to a lower output of work; an excess means B and C being excreted in the urine. Vitamins A, D, E and K are more of a problem because they are fat-soluble and, if taken in excess, can remain as toxins in the liver.

Iodine, calcium, zinc, phosphorus and iron, particularly for women, are minerals that the body needs to obtain in very small amounts and a regular intake can help to achieve this.

Natural sources of vitamins and minerals

Vitamin or mineral	Food source
Vitamin A	Oily fish, meat, eggs, liver, cheese, butter and margarine
Vitamin B_1 (Thiamin)	Wholemeal bread and cereals, liver, kidneys, red meat, pulses (beans, lentils and peas)
Vitamin B_2 (Riboflavin)	Liver, kidneys, red meat, chicken, milk, yoghurt, cheese, eggs
Vitamin C	Fresh fruit (especially citrus), berries and currants, vegetables (especially dark green, leafy vegetables, tomatoes and peppers)
Vitamin D	Sunlight (UV light on the skin), fresh oils and oily fish, eggs, vitamin-D-fortified cereals, margarine and some yoghurts
Vitamin E	Wheatgerm, pure vegetable oils, egg yolk, sunflower seeds, nuts and avocado
Calcium	Milk, cheese, yoghurt, soft bones of small fish, seafood, green leafy vegetables, fortified wheat flour and bread, pulses
Sodium	Table salt, tinned vegetables, fish, meat, bread, cheese
Potassium	Vegetables, fruit juices, unprocessed cereals
Iron	Red meat, liver, offal, fortified breakfast cereals, shellfish, wholegrain bread, pasta and cereals, pulses, green leafy vegetables
Zinc	Meat, eggs, wholegrain cereals, milk and dairy products
Magnesium	Cereals, vegetables, fruit, potatoes, milk
Phosphorous	Cereals, meat, fish, milk and dairy products, green vegetables

Supplements

If you have a hectic lifestyle and often do not eat a balanced diet you may benefit from vitamin and mineral supplements. This is particularly important if you are swimming regularly or competing, and will ensure that you are getting all the nutrients you need each day. Before taking supplements, it would be worth consulting a nutritionist or investing in a book that gives you all the information you need to decide what to take. This is recommended especially for female swimmers if you think you may be anaemic. There is no hard evidence to suggest that vitamins will improve your actual performance, but they do form part of the total picture.

Snacks

If you need to squeeze in your training either early in the morning or at lunchtime, you should be aware of the advantage of quick snacks to replenish lost energy. Don't use snacks to replace meals. However, glycogen in the muscles needs replacing rapidly after exercise and this can be achieved by eating a snack with plenty of quick-release carbohydrate. This is particularly important if you have swum early in the morning and have to work for the rest of the day.

Snacks can be quite simple but may need a little preparation before you go swimming. The following are some suggestions that you might like to keep in your bag or arrange to keep at work so that you are able to snack as required:

- banana sandwich (2 slices of bread and 1 banana)
- 2 scotch pancakes
- 2 cereal bars and a carton of flavoured milk
- carton of low-fat rice pudding
- toast with honey (2 slices)
- peanut butter sandwich
- fresh fruit and low-fat yoghurt.

Losing weight

Carrying the right amount of weight is important for anyone who is training. You should look to cut down on body fat and yet have sufficient reserves to be able to complete all the training you are planning to undertake. You can achieve this by creating a negative energy balance, that is by taking in fewer calories than you use up. You can lose weight either by reducing your calorie intake or by increasing your physical activity – in this case swimming – or through a combination of both.

As well as reducing your body fat percentage, it is important to maintain both muscle mass and strength in order to train. Therefore, you should aim to lose only one to two pounds of fat per week. If you start losing more than this, you may be losing some of your lean tissue. If this happens you should look to increase the amount you are eating by between 250 and 500 calories per day in order to be able to train sensibly. If you are serious about combining swimming with losing weight, it would be useful to keep a daily diary of what you eat. To lose one pound in weight a week you need to have a calorie deficit of about 500 calories a day.

Pages 99–100 provide some examples of meals that you might eat over a week that, when combined with swimming, will help towards losing weight sensibly. Don't forget your daily intake of water as well.

Competition diet

If you are thinking about taking part in competitions you will need to give special thought to your nutrition. What and how you eat can mean the difference between winning and losing, or performing at your own personal best. The following offers some basic advice.

Generally speaking, in the week leading up to competition it is important to fill up your glycogen stores and to keep well hydrated. So, eat plenty of carbohydrate foods (see pages 88–90) and drink plenty of water. It is vital to ensure that you replace muscle glycogen immediately after training in the week prior to competition. If you

Meal	Suggestions
Monday breakfast	1 glass of orange juice 1 cup of porridge oats with 300 ml skimmed milk 1 tablespoon of sultanas or raisins
Monday lunch	1 large baked potato 1 small portion of tuna
Monday dinner	1 piece of grilled chicken 1 portion of garden peas 1 portion of cabbage
Tuesday breakfast	1 carton of low-fat yoghurt 2 scrambled eggs 1 glass of orange juice
Tuesday lunch	1 bowl of pasta salad 1 portion of olive oil dressing 1 muesli bar
Tuesday dinner	1 cod fillet 6 yellow and red cherry tomatoes handful of basil small portion of grated Parmesan cheese
Wednesday breakfast	1 glass of apple juice 2 poached eggs
Wednesday lunch	1 bagel 1 small portion of low-fat cheese spread 1 handful of mixed nuts
Wednesday dinner	1 piece of baked turkey 3 carrots 2 parsnips
Thursday breakfast	1 glass of orange juice 1 bowl of muesli 300 ml skimmed milk 1 slice of wholegrain toast
Thursday lunch	1 baked potato 1 portion of sweetcorn
Thursday dinner	1 bulb of roast fennel cooked with 6 cherry tomatoes, pitted black olives and garlic in olive oil

Friday breakfast	1 glass of apple juice 2 shredded wheat 300 ml skimmed milk 1 banana
Friday lunch	2 slices of light wheat bread 2 slices of turkey 1 apple
Friday dinner	1 poached salmon fillet on bed of short-grain rice 1 portion of petit pois
Saturday breakfast	1 glass of orange juice 2 slices of wholegrain toast 2 teaspoons of honey 1 carton of low-fat yoghurt
Saturday lunch	1 leg of cooked chicken 1 large handful of dried fruits other than nuts
Saturday dinner	1 small portion of tagliatelle pasta 1 parsnip fresh rosemary and thyme 1 garlic clove 3 slices of pancetta
Sunday breakfast	1 cup of porridge oats 1 tablespoon of raisins 300 ml skimmed milk 2 slices of wholegrain toast 2 teaspoons of honey
Sunday lunch	1 bowl of mixed salad with peppers 1 banana
Sunday dinner	1 grilled sea bass with lemon 1 portion of spinach 1 portion of kale

don't, you will enter the race with low energy stores and at a distinct disadvantage, and this will almost certainly lead to poor performance. Exact quantities will depend upon the type of event you are competing in (short-duration events such as sprints, or long- duration endurance events).

On the day of competition your main aims will be to top up glycogen stores in the liver, keep well hydrated, ensure that your blood sugar levels are maintained and stave off hunger. You will need to eat at least one main meal (high in carbohydrates) before competition. This needs to be 2–4 hours before your first race so that your stomach is empty and your blood sugar levels have normalised. Avoid heavy eating immediately before and between races. Remember to drink plenty of water. If you find a meal that works particularly well for you then stick to it and keep to your routine. This will most likely help your performance physically and mentally.

High or moderate GI carbohydrates that are more liquid and easily digestible are recommended before competition at the expense of protein and fats. Fatty foods take too much time to digest, while simple carbohydrates such as glucose and dextrose are not really suitable as they cause blood sugar levels to rise and fall very quickly, leaving the body feeling weak. Tea and coffee contain caffeine, which is a stimulant and will increase your heart rate and interfere with focus and relaxation. They are also diuretics and will increase urine output and lead to dehydration. They should be avoided prior to competition.

Here are some useful foods to eat before, during and after you race:

The night before	■ pasta or rice dishes with tomato-based sauces ■ water
Two to four hours before	■ cereal and low-fat milk, bread, toasted sandwiches, rolls, potatoes ■ water
One hour before	■ energy or sports nutrition bar ■ dried apricots ■ water
15–30 minutes before	■ water ■ sports drink
Between heats	■ sports drink ■ meal replacement products ■ bananas ■ rice cakes, energy bars, rolls
Post-competition	■ sports drinks ■ energy bars ■ pasta/rice dishes ■ pizza

6 Taking it further

How to begin?

Let's imagine that so far, you have been swimming for fun or fitness – but now you would like to try for one or two competitions. How do you go about it? Probably the best approach would be to contact the ASA (see p. 117 for contact details) and ask to speak to the Membership Services Department. The ASA keeps a comprehensive list of clubs and county secretaries and will probably put you in touch with your local representative. They will be able to advise you on the clubs available, where they train and the days on which they meet. There are also some handy ASA leaflets on Masters swimming that include useful tips for when you enter your first competitions.

One interesting point to be aware of is that many former world record holders and Olympic champions do take part in Masters competitions – particularly in the USA, where they have more such champions anyway. As a result, it is easy to rub shoulders with and meet stars of the past, even if they are competing in much faster heats of the same event than yours. By comparison, this happens to a much smaller extent in veterans' athletics. One of the endearing features of Masters swimming is that top swimmers can and do mix with average ones.

Trying something new raises lots of questions, and in this case some of them might be:

'How fast do I need to be to take part?'
The answer is that you generally don't need to be very fast – Masters swimming sees itself as the epitome of the Corinthian swimming spirit. Fast swimmers do take part, but they tend not to intimidate the less speedy performers.

'How often do I need to train to attain a reasonable level for Masters competitions?'
There is no set distance but as a guide four sessions a week of about one hour, aiming to complete 2500–3000 m per session, would be a realistic target. If possible, swim and enter competitions with a partner.

'What type of structure exists for competitions?'
There is a progression to the structure that makes it easier for a swimmer to build into the system. You can start in county events then move to open competitions (i.e. ones in which anyone can take part), then on to national and finally international open events.

'Do I need to have competed before as a young swimmer?'
The answer to this one is a clear no. You do not have to be a very experienced swimmer to take part. In fact, many Masters swimmers comment that they are faster in their later years than when they were at school.

Masters swimming

There is a huge amount of interest in Masters swimming across the UK; the Amateur Swimming Association has a list of about 400 clubs that are involved – both existing swimming clubs with a Masters section, and dedicated Masters swimming clubs (in all, numbering some

5000 members). An ASA National Masters Committee advises on grass roots development as well as promoting competitive opportunities, and each of the ASA Districts has a District Secretary with responsibility for Masters swimming in their area.

Masters swimming is designed to offer opportunities for competition at all levels on all strokes. According to the rules of FINA (the world governing body): 'The Masters programme shall promote fitness, friendships and understanding through swimming, diving, synchronised swimming, water polo and open-water swimming among those competitors with a minimum age limit of 25 years'. The movement is now worldwide, making it possible for adult swimmers to compete all year round in different parts of the world against people of similar age. Age groups are split into the following years: 19–24, 25–29, 30–34, 35–39, 40–44, 45–49, 50–54, 55–59, 60–64, 65–69, 70–74, 75–79, 80–84, and 85 and over. For record purposes, the age groups extend to 85–89, 90–94, 95–100, and – amazingly – 100–104. Normally, heats of competitions are seeded from slowest to fastest, making it possible for people of the same standard to compete against one another. There are generally no qualifying times to enter. Anyone can take part, however slow.

In relay races, FINA lays down rules requiring the team entry to be based on the total age of the team (based on whole years): 100–119, 120–159, 160–199, 200–239, 240–279, 280–319, 320–359 years and then in 40-year increments going up as high as necessary. They also allow for age groups to be combined, whether swimmers are competing individually or as a team. This means that no one need compete in their age group on their own if they are the only entry for an event.

The first Masters swimming competition with ASA approval was held at the City University Swimming Pool in London in 1971, when the author and a group of enthusiasts from Otter Swimming Club got together to organise a competition for British swimmers. We copied the US format of age groups, although the oldest group only went up to 65 years! Nearly 200 people took part and the

Masters movement in Britain was born. The first ASA National Masters Competition was introduced in 1981 and the first European Masters at Blackpool in 1987. In recent years, the World Masters has been held in places as far apart as Brisbane, Rio de Janeiro, Indianapolis and Montreal.

There are two types of Masters competition: short-course and long-course. The short-course competitions are held in pools of 25 metres or smaller, and the long-course ones in 50-metre pools. The long-course events are much more tiring, for obvious reasons!

What Masters swimming can mean to you

Why, then, would you take part in Masters swimming? There are a number of reasons:

- as a competitive outlet
- as a form of enjoyment
- to create friendships and socialise
- as an opportunity to travel and meet people
- if you have previously been a competitive swimmer, as an opportunity to reacquaint with friends
- to experience once again the excitement of competing that you felt in younger years.

Many pools that have fitness sessions claim that the friendships made there last for years. For example, at the ASA Swim Scheme at Crystal Palace National Sports Centre, an adult fitness session takes place in the 25 m pool each week. The organisers maintain that some of the swimmers have been both attending and friends for years. About 40 swimmers are split into two lanes according to speed. They start with stretching exercises on the poolside before entering the water. Some of the swimmers use these sessions to build up their water work as triathletes.

Families can also take part together. There are many examples of husband and wife, mother and daughter and father and son combinations taking part in the same competition or training session. For instance, Sue Shrimpton, who swam for Britain at the 1968 Mexico

Olympics, holds British Masters Records over 50 and 100 m freestyle in the 45–9 years age group – with times not much slower than when she was competing for Britain. Her mother, Doreen Cope, often competed in the same Masters competitions and holds British Masters Records in the 70–4 year group.

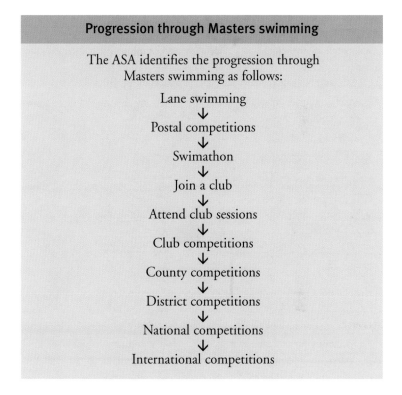

Progression through Masters swimming

The ASA identifies the progression through Masters swimming as follows:

Lane swimming
↓
Postal competitions
↓
Swimathon
↓
Join a club
↓
Attend club sessions
↓
Club competitions
↓
County competitions
↓
District competitions
↓
National competitions
↓
International competitions

Masters swimming in the UK and abroad

There are a number of major competitions that are held each year in both the UK and abroad. FINA provides a full list of competitions listing the month in which the event is normally held, the length of pool (in yards or metres) and the venue of the event as a guide. Some of the events will be fixed; others will move from place to place each year. A full list of these events can be obtained from www.fina.org.

Whatever event you are aiming for, remember that if you are competing abroad as an individual, you need to inform the ASA. It is also important to keep all of your competition performances as well as details about the venue in your training diary. In the UK, the ASA Masters Championships rotate annually within the ASA districts, but due to the rising number of competitors (over 1000), the competition has recently been held in pools large enough to cope with this increased number.

Masters swimming has continued to expand throughout the world. In Europe alone, 29 countries now hold competitions. More than 20,440 competitors took part in the 1999 national championships of each of these countries. At the IX World Masters Championships in Riccione in 2004, more than 8000 swimmers took part.

In April 2000, the first ever National Masters Conference was held in Britain as part of an effort to improve communications. Recent introductions into the programme include a half-hour national Masters postal swim, the compilation of top-ten ranking lists as an incentive for people to improve, and a national Masters survey. Races for swimmers between the ages of 19 and 24 or 20 and 24 are becoming increasingly popular.

The competitive programme

In terms of events and distances, there is plenty of scope. The table on p. 109 shows the full international competitive programme.

To progress according to your own goals, you need to create a swimming strategy – this is important for both your training and your racing. The first thing is to take a long-term view: given that strategy is all about where you are now, where you want to be in the future and how you are going to get there, a long-term perspective is important. Remind yourself of your overall goals, and of the objectives of your swimming programme. Are you training to compete in Masters swimming at the very highest level? Do you just want to maintain a certain level of fitness – or to compete in order

Events featured in the full international Masters programme

Individual				
Freestyle (m)	Backstroke (m)	Breaststroke (m)	Butterfly (m)	Individual medley (m)
50	50	50	50	
100	100	100	100	100
200	200	200	200	200
400				400
800				
1500				
Relays				
Freestyle (m)	Backstroke (m)	Breaststroke (m)	Butterfly (m)	Individual medley (m)
200				200
200 (mixed)				200 (mixed)

to maintain similar times to those you held previously, despite the passing of the years? These are all perfectly valid reasons for taking part, but different goals will determine the way in which you proceed. Ask your club for advice on setting your targets, and remember to build up to these gradually, breaking your season into phases.

As discussed in Chapter 4, you should be looking to come to two peaks in the year – for the short-course season in October, and for the long-course season in June. Your peaks should last for a period of two or three days at most, and during the rest of the season you will not be able to record times close to these peaks.

Following are some examples of how you might slowly reduce your training times over the year in order to reach your target in a progressive way. Note the peaks in October and June. There is obviously no formula for this, so use the figures as a guideline only for planning your season – and refer to Chapter 4 for advice on planning and devising your schedules.

Sample progressions – 100 m freestyle

Month	Target time: 1:30	Target time: 1:20	Target time: 1:10	Target time: 1:00
January	1:50	1:40	1:30	1:15
February	1:50	1:40	1:30	1:15
March	1:45	1:35	1:25	1:09
April	1:45	1:35	1:25	1:09
May	1:35	1:26	1:15	1:05
June	1:30	1:20	1:10	1:00
July	1:33	1:21	1:11	1:01
August	1:36	1:24	1:14	1:04
September	1:36	1:24	1:14	1:04
October	1:33	1:21	1:11	1:01
November	1:45	1:35	1:25	1:10
December	1:45	1:35	1:25	1:10

Sample progressions – 100 m backstroke

Month	Target time: 1:40	Target time: 1:25	Target time: 1:15	Target time: 1:10
January	2:00	1:45	1:35	1:25
February	2:00	1:45	1:35	1:25
March	1:50	1:35	1:25	1:20
April	1:46	1:30	1:20	1:15
May	1:45	1:29	1:19	1:14
June	1:40	1:25	1:15	1:10
July	1:41	1:26	1:16	1:11
August	1:43	1:28	1:18	1:13
September	1:45	1:29	1:19	1:14
October	1:41	1:26	1:14	1:11
November	1:50	1:40	1:30	1:22
December	1:50	1:40	1:30	1:22

Sample progressions – 100 m butterfly

Month	Target time: 1:40	Target time: 1:25	Target time: 1:15	Target time: 1:10
January	2:00	1:45	1:35	1:25
February	2:00	1:45	1:35	1:25
March	1:50	1:35	1:25	1:20
April	1:46	1:30	1:20	1:15
May	1:47	1:31	1:19	1:14
June	1:40	1:25	1:15	1:10
July	1:41	1:26	1:16	1:11
August	1:43	1:28	1:18	1:13
September	1:45	1:30	1:20	1:15
October	1:41	1:26	1:16	1:11
November	1:50	1:40	1:30	1:22
December	1:50	1:40	1:30	1:22

Sample progressions – 100 m breaststroke

Month	Target time: 1:40	Target time: 1:30	Target time: 1:20	Target time: 1:15
January	2:05	1:50	1:40	1:30
February	2:00	1:50	1:40	1:30
March	1:55	1:45	1:30	1:25
April	1:50	1:37	1:25	1:20
May	1:49	1:38	1:26	1:21
June	1:45	1:38	1:20	1:15
July	1:46	1:39	1:21	1:16
August	1:48	1:41	1:23	1:18
September	1:47	1:42	1:24	1:16
October	1:46	1:39	1:21	1:16
November	2:00	1:45	1:35	1:25
December	2:00	1:45	1:35	1:25

Training before a competition

The period before a competition always requires a different form of training as you prepare for the mental as well as physical battle ahead. Here are some of the things you need to do:

- decrease distances swum
- increase pace of swims
- decrease number of repetitions swum
- rest as much as possible between training sessions in order to let the body recover from a build-up of training effects
- ease back on strength training
- maintain high levels of flexibility training
- focus mental approach on performing at a high level in the forth-coming event
- sleep as much as possible
- sharpen up on starts and turns
- visualise a race situation and mentally prepare for it.

Preparing for a race – the taper period

During the taper period, you should ease off in preparation for com-petition. The aim is to achieve both physical relaxation and mental alertness. The tapering process can vary from swimmer to swimmer: generally, it calls for longer rests between repetitions, fewer training sessions, slightly shorter distances in order to sharpen up, and more sleep. These factors combine to bring you to your peak.

Knowing how much tapering you need requires considerable prac-tice, especially since this varies widely from person to person. The only way you can determine what suits you is to try out different variations. Sometimes swimmers rest up too much and find that they have lost some of the crucial endurance-based fitness that they had built up during training. This might manifest itself in poor per-formance over, say, the last 30 m of a 100 m race. On the other hand, there are swimmers who do not rest enough, and find that they are too tired and insufficiently sharp when they compete.

Some swimmers like a long taper that lasts for a number of weeks; others prefer just two or three days. Yet another approach is to go the other way. In the month before competition, the swimmer 'overdoes' their training, increasing the workload by 30–40 per cent. They then taper from this increased workload.

There is a fine dividing line between what works for you and what doesn't, and trial and error is often the only way to find out. As a general guide, swimmers taking part in longer races do not need as much taper time as sprinters. Sprinting, being an explosive event, requires more rest. In addition, you will need to make a judgement based on the number of races you are taking part in during a competition. If you have a long taper, your performances are likely to drop more quickly in a competition where you have a whole number of races on different days. In such cases, you may need a much shorter taper. Chapter 4 gives more specific advice about tailoring your training programme towards your peaks.

Race day

You have been looking forward to this day for many months. Avoid ruining it with poor application and an unplanned approach. Here is some general advice for race-day preparation.

- Make sure that you get a good night's sleep the night before and get up reasonably early so your metabolism will be working well.
- Your breakfast should contain plenty of carbohydrate, some proteins but little fat, as fats take time to digest. If you are racing in the afternoon, ensure that you eat a main meal (high in carbohydrates) at least 2 hours before the start of the race.
- Take a short walk before your race, to work any stiffness out of your system.

'I swim for about 40 minutes six times a week. It keeps me fit and is the best stress-buster I know. I love the challenge of improving my technique and I always leave the pool feeling better than when I arrived.'

Professor Tom Hanahoe

- When you arrive at the swimming meeting, make sure you have a good warm-up. This should consist of anything between half an hour to an hour's swimming in which you also practise starts and turns.
- Remember to take water every hour to prevent dehydration.
- Wrap up warm – and that particularly includes wearing training shoes to prevent loss of body heat through the soles of the feet.
- Carry out your due diligence in terms of knowing where everything is, including the warm-up pool, reporting area, etc. Make sure you know your reporting time and your event number
- There is one further useful tip before you race. When awaiting their event, swimmers usually sit in a row of seats behind the start. At this point in time, swim the race through in your mind, remembering all the key points about starting and turning and finishing the race with the arms at long reach. This thought process should help to build the adrenalin at the right time – just before you go into your race. Swim the race through earlier, and the adrenalin necessary for the race will have come and gone.

Open-water swimming

Nowadays, there are only a few Channel swims made each year. Hazardous and overcrowded shipping conditions have made it difficult for the Captain Webbs of today! Long-distance or open-water swimming is, however, something that you can do into later life. James Counsilman, who was Mark Spitz's coach at Indiana University, swam the English Channel when he was 58 years old.

You don't have to swim the Channel to take part in long-distance swimming, though: there are many shorter swims, and the steady pace of the races combined with the fresh air make this an attractive alternative to pool swimming.

Open-water swimming is a discipline involving competitions of up to 25 km in any outdoor body of water – lakes, rowing courses, seas and reservoirs. The first Open Water World Championships were held in Hawaii in October 2000; and, as a recent development, a Great Britain Open Water Grand Prix has been introduced, with events ranging from 4–10 km in length. These take place between May and October.

Tips and training

Training consists of a structured pool schedule with an emphasis on over-distance swims. This is mainly in the form of long aerobic swims, although a strong speed base is also essential. As far as preparation is concerned, it is sometimes better to make short, frequent training swims or shorter open-water races early in the year in order to build up to the longer races later on.

The most essential skill specific to this kind of swimming is the ability to go in a straight line without any guide to follow. This can be learned by practising lifting your head every so often – to breathe and to look where you are going. The ability to swim in opposing conditions, i.e. wind and waves, can only be developed with experience. This can be conquered to some extent by learning to breathe on both sides, which enables you to breathe away from the approaching waves or wind.

Safety considerations

Safety factors have to be considered in this kind of swimming. Some homework in order to build a fuller knowledge of the area of water, regulations, weather and tidal reports will help to avoid dangers. Swimmers should avoid training in waters where fast craft are present. Most important of all, swimmers should never train alone without an observer. The use of a brightly coloured hat will help an observer spot you. And finally, you should always be aware of the risk of hypothermia – this dangerous condition occurs when too much heat is lost through the body. Low skin-surface temperatures can cause discomfort, but it is only when core temperatures drop that danger arises. Take the appropriate precautions: when in doubt, consult your club or your local ASA representative.

7 Further information

This chapter is intended to help you to find more information to support your training programme.

Swimming associations

Amateur Swimming Association, Harold Fern House, Derby Square, Loughborough, Leicestershire, LE11 5AL
T: 01509 618700
F: 01509 618701
W: www.britishswimming.org

Department for Culture, Media and Sport, 2–4 Cockspur Street, London, SW1Y 5DH
T: 020 7211 6200
E: enquiries@culture.gov.uk
W: www.culture.gov.uk

Scottish Swimming, National Swimming Academy, University of Stirling, Stirling, FK9 4LA
T: 01786 466520
F: 01786 466521
E: info@scottishswimming.com
W: www.scottishswimming.com

Sport England, 3rd Floor, Victoria House, Bloomsbury Square, London, WC1B 4SE
T: 08458 508508
F: 020 7383 5740
E: info@sportengland.org
W: www.sportengland.org

Sport Scotland, Caledonia House, South Gyle, Edinburgh, EH12 9DQ
T: 0131 317 7200
F: 0131 317 7202
W: www.sportscotland.org.uk

Sports Council For Wales, National Sports Centre For Wales, Sophia Gardens, Cardiff, CF1 9SW
T: 029 2030 0500
F: 029 2030 0600
W: www.sports-council-wales.co.uk

Ulster Region Swim Ireland, House of Sport, Upper Malone Road, Belfast, N. Ireland, BT9 5LA
T: 028 90 383807
F: 028 90 682757
W: www.swim-ulster.com

Welsh Amateur Swimming
Association, Welsh National Pool,
Sketty Lane, Swansea, SA2 8QG
T: 01792 513636
F: 01792 513637
W: www.welshasa.co.uk

Information on where to swim

Institute of Sport and Recreation Management, Sir John Beckwith Centre for Sport, Loughborough University, Loughborough, Leicestershire, LE11 3TU
T: 01509 226474
F: 01509 226475
E: info@isrm.co.uk
W: www.isrm.co.uk

Swimming injuries

Association of Chartered Physiotherapists in Sports Medicine, c/o Sandra Barley, 5 Ewden House, 12 Holyrood Avenue, Lodge Moor, Sheffield, S10 4NW
T: 0114 230 5665
W: www.acpsm.org

British Association of Sport and Exercise Medicine, 30 Devonshire Street, London, W1E 6PU
W: www.basem.co.uk

National Sports Medicine Institute of the UK, 32 Devonshire Street, London, W1G 6PU
T: 020 7908 3636
W: www.nsmi.org.uk

Society of Sports Therapists, 16 Royal Terrace, Glasgow, G3 7NY
T: 0845 600 2613
F: 0141 332 5335
W: www.society-of-sports-therapists.org

Visually impaired swimming

British Blind Sport, 4–6 Victoria Terrace, Leamington Spa, Warwickshire, CV31 3AB
T: 08700 789000
F: 08700 789001
E: info@britishblindsport.org.uk
W: www.britishblindsport.org.uk

Deaf swimming

British Deaf Sports Council, 7A Bridge Street, Otley, West Yorkshire, LS21 1BQ
T: 01943 850081
F: 01943 850828
W: www.britishdeafsportscouncil.org.uk

Disabled swimming

Association of British Swimmers with Physical Disabilities, 53 Hawthorn Crescent, Wollaton Park, Nottingham, NG8 1DD
T: 0115 978 3198

British Paralympic Association, 40 Bernard Street, London, WC1N 1ST
T: 020 7211 5222
F: 020 7211 5233
W: www.paralympics.org.uk

Disability Sport England, St Aidan's Church House, Station Road, Ashington, Northumberland, NE63 521496
T: 01670 521496
W: www.disabilitysport.org.uk

Diet

British Nutrition Foundation, High Holborn House, 52–54 High Holborn, London, WC1V 6RQ
T: 020 7404 6504
W: www.nutrition.org.uk

Open-water swimming

Amateur Swimming Association, contact Mike Hemmings, Administrator, Open Water Committee
T: 023 92570865
E: dfytche@asagb.org

British Long Distance Swimming Association, 16 Elmwood Road, Barnton, Norwich, Cheshire, CW8 4NB
T: 01606 75298
W: www.bldsa.org.uk

Channel Crossing Association, Duncan Tyler, Bolden's Wood, Fiddling Lane, Stowting, Ashford, Kent, TN25 6AP
T: 01303 812011
W: www.channelcrossingassociation.com

Channel Swimming Association, Alison Read, Little Gables, Woodhill Road, Sandon, Chelmsford, Essex, CM2 7SF

T: 01245 473581
W: www.channelswimmingassociation.com

Long distance swimming event details: Ali38crossings@aol.com
Maurice.Ferguson@virgin.net

Magazines and publications

Aquazone, c/o Swimming

Peak Performance, 67–71 Gosditch Rd, London, EV1V 7EP
T: 020 7954 3426
E: pp@pponline.co.uk
W: www.pponline.co.uk

Swim News, 356 Sumach Street, Toronto, Ontario, Canada, M4X 1V4
T: 001 416 963 5599
E: swimnews@swimnews.com
W: www.swimnews.com

Swimming, 41 Granby Street, Loughborough, Leicestershire, LE11 3DU
T: 01509 632230
E: swimmingtimes@swimming.org

Swimming World and Swimming Technique, Sports Publications, PO Box 20337, Sedona, AZ 86341, USA
T: 001 800 511 3029
F: 001 800 522 0744
W: www.swiminfo.com

Wavelength, ASA Newsletter, c/o Amateur Swimming Association
T: 01509 618756
E: Helen@asag.org.uk

Books

The Complete Guide to Exercise in Water (2nd edition) by Debbie Lawrence (A & C Black, 2004)

The Complete Guide to Sports Nutrition (4th edition) by Anita Bean (A & C Black, 2003)

The Complete Guide to Strength Training (3rd edition) by Anita Bean (A & C Black, 2004)

The Fit Swimmer, 120 Workouts and Tips by Marianne Brems (Contemporary Books, 1984)

The Handbook of Swimming by David Wilkie and Kelvin Juba (Pelham Books, 1986)

Know The Game Swimming (3rd edition) (A & C Black, 2003)

The Science of Winning by J. Olbrect, 2000 (through Swimshop, 3 Dencora Way, Luton, LU3 3HP, T: 01582 562111, E: swimshopuk@aol.com)

Swimming Coaching by Joseph Dixon (Crowood Press, 1996)

Swimming Drills For Every Stroke by Ruben Guzman (Human Kinetics, 1998)

Swimming Dynamics: Winning Techniques and Strategies by Cecil Colwin (Masters Press, 1998)

Swimming Even Faster by Ernest W. Maglischo (Mayfield Publishing, 1982)

Swimming For Fitness by George Austin and Jim Noble (ASA Publications, 1990)

Swimming Into The 21st Century by Cecil M. Colwin (Human Kinetics, 1992)

Adult Swim Fit Award Scheme

ASA Awards Centre, Unit 1, Kingfisher Enterprise Park, 50 Arthur Street, Redditch, Worcestershire, B98 8LG
T: 0800 220292
F: 01527 514277
E: salesawards@swimming.org
W: www.asa-awards.co.uk

Masters swimming

Masters Aquatic Coaches Association
W: www.macacoach.org

Masters swimming clubs throughout the world
W: www.swimsearch.com

United States Masters Swimming, W: www.usms.org

Index